Arthur Reader

Fishes, Flowers, & Fire as Elements and Deities

In the Phallic faiths & worship of the ancient Religions

Arthur Reader

Fishes, Flowers, & Fire as Elements and Deities
In the Phallic faiths & worship of the ancient Religions

ISBN/EAN: 9783337112332

Printed in Europe, USA, Canada, Australia, Japan

Cover: Foto ©ninafisch / pixelio.de

More available books at **www.hansebooks.com**

FISHES, FLOWERS, AND FIRE WORSHIP.

Fishes, Flowers, & Fire

AS

ELEMENTS AND DEITIES

IN THE

Phallic Faiths & Worship

OF THE

ANCIENT RELIGIONS

OF

Greece, Babylon, Rome, India, &c.

WITH

ILLUSTRATIVE MYTHS AND LEGENDS.

PRIVATELY PRINTED.

A. READER, ORANGE STREET, RED LION SQUARE, LONDON.

1890.

PREFACE.

THE volume now in the reader's hands forms the fifth, and, for the present, the concluding portion of the "Phallic Series" it was found necessary to issue in further explication of certain matters set forth in the first book on this peculiar subject.

Having dealt with Sex Worship generally, Ophiolatræia, the Round Towers and Holed Stones, Trees, Fishes, Flowers, and Fire, the ground has been pretty well covered, and with the exception of an Appendix, which future demands may possibly call forth, the subject is now complete. It is confidently expected that the present volume will be found equally interesting with those which have preceded it; it opens up entirely new matter, and contains a number of curious traditions not before alluded to.

FISHES, FLOWERS, AND FIRE.

CHAPTER I.

FEW, if any, symbols are of such frequent occurrence
among the relics of bygone ages as that of the fish.
Whether we look upon the monuments of Babylon and Nineveh,
upon the walls of the Roman Catacombs where the early
Christians sought a refuge from the fury of their Pagan
persecutors, or amongst the heraldic devices adopted by our
ancestors as coats of arms in comparatively modern times,
the fish is ever prominent. With regard to the latter, it is
certainly remarkable to what an extent it prevails, and
several writers on Heraldry (particularly Moule) have given
us very full accounts and graphic illustrations of its use.
Nor is it one kind of fish only we find thus employed, which
might perhaps be associated with some special myth or
tradition—the dolphin, the herring, the salmon, the trout, the
pike, the barbel, the roach, the sole, the turbot, the flounder,
the haddock, the cod, the hake, the ling, the whiting, the
mullet, the grayling and others have all been pressed into
the same service, and even the different modes of taking fish
by the spear, the net, or the hook, are found in the
armorial ensigns of the lords of manors deriving revenue from
the produce of the fishery. "The boats," says Moule, "employed in the same service, which were at the command of
the sovereign in time of war, and formed the original navy
of Britain, distinguish the ensigns of the maritime lords, and
the corporate bodies to whom the jurisdiction of the ports
was entrusted." B

It is not unlikely that the vast numbers of fishes and their great variety may have had much to do with their employment in this connection; some years ago the British Museum contained fifteen hundred different species, while the museum in Paris—one unusually rich in specimens of this part of the animal kingdom—possessed as many as five thousand, a number which has steadily gone on increasing. "As the symbol of a name, almost all fish have been used in Heraldry; and in many instances fish have been assumed in arms in reference to the produce of the estate, giving to the quaint device a twofold interest. They are borne upright and extended, and when feeding are termed devouring; Allumé, when their eyes are bright, and Parné when their mouths are open." *

"The earliest known device of fish, the zodiacal sign, is emblematical of the fishery of the Nile, commencing in the month of February, about the time when the sun enters Pisces, which is the best season for fishing, according to Pliny. Modern travellers relate that the walls of the temple of Denderah are literally covered with magnificent sculpture and painting. The figures representing the Zodiac are on the ceiling of the portico, and are engraved in the great work on Egypt published by order of the French Government. The signs of the Zodiac were frequently sculptured on the exterior of ancient churches, presenting a sort of rural calendar for the labours of the field each month in the year, which was of practical use.

'When in the Zodiac the fish wheel round,
They loose the floods and irrigate the ground.'

"In his directions to the husbandman for the month of February, old Tusser says:

'To the coast, man, ride, Lent stuff provide;'
with another couplet in encouragement of the fisherman,

'The land doth will, the sea doth wish,
Spare sometimes flesh, and feed off fish.'

"The Zodiacal signs also appear as an ornament on antique vases, coins, pavements, &c., and are painted in bright colours on the inside of several mummy cases now in the British Museum. A manuscript in the Cottonian Library shows the sign Pisces having a connecting line from the tail of each fish." *

* Moule's Heraldry.

On many churches and other buildings both in England and on the continent the same device is found. The porch of the Virgin at Notre Dame at Paris has a number of compartments representing the zodiacal signs and the labours of the different months. The doorway of the church of St. Margaret, York, is similarly adorned, as is one of the porches of Merton College, Oxford. The western doorway of Iffley Church, said to be one of the most beautiful specimens of Anglo-Norman architecture in England, bears the sign of the fishes.

In Canterbury Cathedral also is a pavement of large stones, somewhat rudely inlaid, bearing figures of the zodiacal signs in circular compartments. The fishes are attached by a line passing from mouth to mouth.

In the Roman Catacombs the fish is frequently found amongst the countless inscriptions with which the walls are crowded. Maitland describes it as there found as a symbol expressive of the name of Christ, and remarkable as affording a combination of everything desirable in a tessera, or mystic sign. The Greek for fish, ιχθυς, contains the initials of Ιησους, Χριστος Θεου Υιος Σωτηρ: Jesus Christ, Son of God, the Saviour; a sentence which had been adopted from the sibylline verses. Moreover the phonetic sign of this word, the actual fish, was an emblem whose meaning was entirely concealed from the uninitiated: an important point with those who were surrounded by foes ready to ridicule and blaspheme whatever of Christianity they could detect. Nor did the appropriateness of the symbol stop here. "The fish," observed Tertullian, "seems a fit emblem of Him whose spiritual children are, like the offspring of fishes, born in the water of baptism."*

"On walls, as well as tombstones, we find the Fish, Phœnix, Anchor, Ship, Olive and Palm, all of which are sacred to the God of Fertility or the procreative energies. The fish, we are told, was adopted by those Christians because of the alphabetical rebus—the Greek word I.K.Th.U.S. containing the initial letters of the words forming this title in Greek, 'Jesus Christ, Son of God, Saviour;' but Ikthus was a holy name in Egypt and the East, long ere Greece had adopted her varied faiths, and long before the good

* Maitland's Church in the Catacombs.

Nazarene had preached his holy gospel in the wilds of
Judea. The Hebrew for fish is Dg, Dag or De-ag, which
some think may have sprung from the Sanscrit De-Dev, and
Ag or Ab, and be allied to the solar Ak, and Aqua,
water. Dagan was the fish-god (Alheim) of the Philistines,
and spelling Dag backwards as was so common and natural,
seeing some peoples read from right to left, and others from
left to right, we get Gad, the good one, that is God or
Goddess of Day, as in Isa. lxv. 11, where, in connection
with Meni the moon, we read : 'Ye are they that prepare
a table for Gad, and that furnish the offering unto Meni;'
which Bagster's Comprehensive Bible admits to be stars or
such objects. Dag, says Calmet, signifies Preserver, and so
Saviour, which has many ancient connections with fish and
water, as we see in the case of Dagon. St. Augustine said
of Christ : 'He is the great Fish that lives in the midst
of the waters;' so no wonder that Ichthus, a fish, should
become a holy term, and applied to Christ's representative,
who in token wears a Poitrine as his higher officers wear
what is called a mitre or turban like a fish's mouth.
Christ, being a Hebrew, of course received the title Ikthus
from his Greek followers, just as he got I.H.S.—the mono-
gram of Bacchus—from those who forsook that god to
follow Christianity. There is nothing sacred about such
matters. Ich or Ik, or Ak = Ab, at once Our Father and
water; and in India the fish is the god of the water, and
so we have Dev-ab, from which may come Deg-an or Dagon.
The Greeks, of course, used Thus or theus, and so Ik-theus
or God-Ik; at any rate Christians have made Ik-thus a
veritable God, and water its element a very holy thing.
The most ancient Keltic tongues seem to identify the two,
for water in Gaelic is Uisge, the water of life being
Wisge (whiskey), and a fish Iasg, or in old Irish, Iska or
Ischa, which is an Eastern term for Jesus. If V or F—
the digamma—is here admissible, then we arrive very near
our own word Fish. Perhaps Vishnoo, Viçnu or Fishnoo,
is responsible here, for he is the first who rises out of
the water, and from a fish; and from his first incarnation
to his last, he is always connected with both." *

"Fish" says Moule, "have often been made the vehicle

* Forlong.

of religious instruction, and for this purpose all the fine arts have been put in requisition. Amongst many pictures by the first masters in which the finny tribe are introduced, that of Saint Anthony, of Padua, preaching to the fish, may be mentioned. This fine picture, by Salvator Rosa, is in the collection at Althorp House, in Northamptonshire; the sermon itself is given in Addison's Travels in Italy.

"On the conventual seal of Glastonbury Abbey are represented the figures of Saint Dunstan between Saint Patrick and Saint Benignus; each has his emblem beneath his feet; the last has a party of fish: perhaps, adds the historian of the abbey, he also preached to them, as Saint Anthony did.

"A fish furnishing the University of Cambridge with a religious feast was the occasion of a tract, entitled 'Vox Piscis; or, the Book-fish;' containing three treatises which were found inside a cod fish in Cambridge market, on Midsummer Eve, 1676. This fish is said to have been taken in Lynn deeps, and after finding a book within it, the fish was carried by the bedel to the vice-chancellor; and coming as it did at the commencement, the very time when good learning and good cheer were most expected, it was quaintly remarked, that this sea guest had brought his book and his carcass to furnish both.

"In the arms of the city of Glasgow, and in those of the ancient see, a salmon with a ring in its mouth is said to record a miracle of St. Kentigern, the founder of the see and the first bishop of Glasgow. On the reverse of Bishop Wishart's seal in the reign of Edward II., this supposed allusion to the legendary story of St. Kentigern appears for the first time.

Some of the early bishops of Glasgow displayed the figure of a salmon, either on the sides of or below the shield of arms on their seals, a circumstance which may be accounted for, without reference to a miracle, as depicting the produce of the Clyde. The revenue of the church of Glasgow at the Reformation included one hundred and sixty-eight salmon arising from the franchise or fishing in that river.

James Cameron, Lord Privy Seal to King James I. of Scotland and bishop of Glasgow in 1462, bore on his episcopal seal the figure of St. Kentigern in a tabernacle,

below which are his paternal arms, three bars, having a
salmon with a ring in its mouth on either side of the shield,
which is surmounted by the mitre. The ring is, perhaps,
a type of the annular money, then current among the
Britons.

"It is curious to note how the emblem of the same
fish has continued to enter into the composition of the
Glasgow arms and those of the ecclesiastical establishment.

"The diocese of Glasgow was erected into an arch-
bishopric in 1491, with Galloway, Argyll and the Isles as
suffragans. James Beaton, archbishop of Glasgow and
abbot of Dumfermline, the uncle of Cardinal Beaton, died
primate of Scotland in 1539. Many munificent marks of
his public spirit and piety long resisted time, and remained
after the cathedral ceremonies had been deserted for the
plain offices of the kirk of Scotland.

"On the walls of the Episcopal Palace or Castle of
Glasgow were sculptured the arms of Beaton—azure, a fess
between three mascles, or, quartered with Balfour, argent,
on a chevron sable and otter's head erased of the first,
and below the shield, a salmon with a ring in its mouth,
as represented on the seals of his predecessors.

"Another Archbishop Beaton re-founded the Scotch
College at Paris in 1603, where, as a monument to his
memory, are his arms, surmounted by the episcopal hat,
and beneath the shield the fish and ring, the emblem of
the see of Glasgow. In more recent times Archbishop
Cairncross, in 1684, bore the arms of the see impaled with
his paternal coat.

"The arms of the city of Glasgow are those of the
former see, argent, on a mount a tree with a bird on a
branch to the dexter, and a bell pendent on the sinister
side, the stem of a tree surmounted by a salmon in fess
having in its mouth a gold ring." *

Dr. Dibdin says, "The legend of the 'Fish and the
Ring,' is extant in well nigh every chap-book in Scotland;
old Spotswood is among the earliest historians who garnished
up the dish from the Latin monastic legends, and Messrs.
Smith, Mc.Lellan and Cleland, have not failed to quote his
words. They report of St. Kentigern, that a lady of good

* Moule's Heraldry.

place in the country having lost her ring as she crossed the river Clyde, and her husband waxing jealous, as if she had bestowed the same on one of her lovers, she did mean herself unto Kentigern, entreating his help for the safety of her honour; and that he, going to the river after he had used his devotion, willed one who was making to fish, to bring the first that he caught, which was done. In the mouth of this fish he found the ring, and sending it to the lady, she was thereby freed of her husband's suspicion. The credit of this I believe upon the reporters; but however it be, the see and city of Glasgow do both of them bear in their arms a fish with a ring in its mouth even to this day." *

Moule remarks that "the classical tale of Polycrates, related by Herodotus a thousand years before the time of St. Kentigern, is perhaps the earliest version of the fish and ring, which has often been repeated with variations. The ring, Herodotus says was an emerald set in gold and beautifully engraved, the work of Theodorus the Samian; and this very ring, Pliny relates, was preserved in the Temple of Concord at Rome, to which it was given by the Emperor Augustus. The device of the fish is engraved in M. Claude Paradin's " Hervical Devices " as an emblem of uninterrupted prosperity."

"If we turn to chapter xxxviii. of Mahomet's Koran, we find the story of the fish and the ring in another form. The note upon the words—' We placed on his throne a counterfeit body,' says : ' The most received exposition of this passage is taken from the following Talmudic fable : Solomon, having taken Sidon, and slain the king of that city, brought away his daughter Jerada, who became his favourite; and because she ceased not to lament her father's loss, he ordered the devils to make an image of him for her consolation : which being done, and placed in her chamber, she and her maids worshipped it morning and evening, according to their custom. At length Solomon being informed of this idolatry, which was practised under his roof by his vizier, Asaf, he broke the image, and having chastised the woman went out into the desert, where he wept and made supplications to God; who did not think fit,

* Northern Tour.

however, to let his negligence pass without some correction. It was Solomon's custom, while he washed himself, to entrust his signet, on which his kingdom depended, with a concubine of his named Amina : one day, therefore, when she had the ring in her custody, a devil named Sakhar came to her in the shape of Solomon, and received the ring from her ; by virtue of which he became possessed of the kingdom, and sat on the throne in the shape which he had borrowed, making what alterations in the law he pleased. Solomon, in the mean time, being changed in his outward appearance and known to none of his subjects, was obliged to wander about and beg alms for his subsistence ; till at length, after the space of forty days, which was the time the image had been worshipped in his house, the devil flew away and threw the signet into the sea ; the signet was immediately swallowed by a fish, which being taken and given to Solomon, he found the ring in its belly, and having by this means recovered the kingdom, took Sakhar, and, tying a great stone to his neck, threw him into the lake of Tiberias."

One of the windows of St. Neot's Church, Cornwall, contains the history of that saint known as the pious sacristan of Glastonbury Abbey, "perhaps," says Moule "the only instance of the legend of a local saint so represented, and one of the most splendid specimens of stained glass in the kingdom. The hermit's fish-pond, now remaining in the valley near his cell, afforded materials for one of the legendary tales now represented in the window. In this pool there were three fishes, of which Neot had divine permission to take one every day, with an assurance that the supply should never be diminished. Being afflicted with a severe indisposition, his disciple Barius one day caught two fishes, and having boiled one and broiled the other, placed them before him : ' What hast thou done ?' exclaimed Neot ; ' lo, the favour of God deserts us : go instantly and restore these fishes to the water.' While Barius was absent Neot prostrated himself in earnest prayer, till he returned with the intelligence that the fishes were disporting in the pool. Barius again went and took only one fish, of which Neot had no sooner tasted than he was restored to perfect health."*

* Gorham. Hist. S. Neots.

A species of perch, common in the Mediterranean, is of a brilliant scarlet colour, but with a very strong spinal fin, and, from the resemblance of this spine to a razor, it is named *le barbier*. This fish is held sacred among the divers for marine productions, and when caught by a hook, it is instantly relieved by the rest of the shoal cutting the line of the angler with their sharp spines.

"The dolphin, as a most peculiarly sacred fish, was called Philanthropist by the ancients, and said to delight in music. It saved the great bard Arion when he threw himself into the Mediterranean on his way to Corinth, which event is said to have happened in the seventh century B.C., or about the time the story of Jonah arose. The Greeks placed the dolphin in their Zodiac. Burckhardt says in his travels in Nubia, that no one is permitted to throw a lance at or injure a dolphin in the Red Sea; and the same rule is enforced among most of the Greek islands.

"Neptune, the male sea-god of Rome, was identical with Poseidon of Greece, and his temples and festivals were in the Campus Martius. Poseidon was a brother of Jupiter and Pluto, and a mighty representative god-man of the waters, and of what the sea symbolised; his was the teeming womb of fertility, and therefore woman. His hosts are dolphins and innumerable sea-nymphs and monsters. His chariots are yoked with horses, which he is said to have created and taught men to manage. His symbol is the phallic trident, or rather the Trisool, or 'giver of life' of Siva, which can cleave rocks, produce water, and shake heaven and earth. The Nephthus of Egypt was the goddess of the coasts of the Red Sea and the wife of the wicked serpent deity Typhon. The Dolphin as a highly emblematic fish often stands for Neptune himself, although it probably first rose in importance from a mere punning on the words delphis a dolphin, and delphus the womb, and occasionally the pudenda. Delphax was also a young pig which was occasionally offered to Juno; Delphi was goddess Earth: symbolic chasm, and Delphinius was her Apollo, and from dolphin springs the name Delphin or Dauphin, the eldest son of the King of France." *

* Rivers of Life.

CHAPTER II.

*The Ancient Sacred Fish—Fish Diet and its supposed Effects—
Fish and the Jews—The god Krodo—Oanes—Dagon—The Fish-
god at Nimroud—Khorsabad—Fish Worship in Syria—Temple
of Dagon at Azotus—The Dagon of the Bible—Adramelech—
Abstinence from Fish Food—Ancient Character of Fish Worship
—Paradise Lost—Ths Irish demi-god Phin—The Fish as a
Christian Symbol—Idea involved in Fish Worship—Holy Fish
Ponds—Ancient Caledonian Objections to Fish—Other anti-fish-
eating Nations—Ishtar.*

INMAN remarks that "the fish selected for honour amongst
the ancients was neither flat, globular, nor cylindrical ;
it was more or less oval, and terminated in a forked tail.
In shape it was like the almond, or the 'concha' with the
'nates.' Its open mouth resembles the 'os uteri,' still called
'os tincæ,' or tench's mouth. Ancient priests are represented
as clothed with a fish, the head being the mitre. The fish's
head as a mitre still adorns the heads of Romish bishops.
The fish was sacred to Venus, and was a favourite esculent
among the luxurious Romans. The fish was an emblem of
fecundity. The word *nun*, however, in the Hebrew, signifies
to *sprout, to put forth*, as well as *fish ;* and thus the fish
symbolises the male principle in an active state. The
creature had a very strong symbolic connection with the
worship of Aphrodite, and the Romanists still eat it on
that day of the week called Dies Veneris, Venus' Day."

"At the present time there are certain fish which are
supposed to give greatly increased virile power to those who
eat them. I have (proceeds Inman) indistinct recollection
of a similar fact having been recorded in Athenæus, who
quotes Theophrastus as his authority. The passage is to the
effect, that a diet on a certain fish enabled an Indian
prince to show one hundred proofs of his manhood in a
single day. The same writer mentions goat's flesh as having
something of the same effect. The Assyrian Oannes was
represented as a man-fish, and the Capricorn or goat with
fish tail, in the Zodiac, is said to have been an emblem
of him.

"The fish was also associated with Isis, who, like Venus, represented the female element in creation. It was likewise a sacred emblem amongst the Buddhists.

"Since writing the above, I have ascertained that eating fish for supper, on Friday night, is a Jewish custom or institution. As amongst that nation fecundity is a blessing specially promised by the Omnipotent, so it is thought proper to use human means for ensuring the blessing on the day set apart by the Almighty. The Jewish Sabbath begins at sunset on Friday, and three meals are to be taken during the day, which are supposed to have a powerful aphrodisiac operation. The ingredients are meat and fish, garlic and pepper; and the particular fish selected, so far as I can learn, is the skate—that which in the Isle of Man is still supposed to be a powerful satyrion. The meal is repeated twice on a Saturday. Mons. Lajard bears testimony to the extent of this custom in the following passage, though he does not directly associate it with the fish, except that the latter are often seen on coins, with the other attributes of Venus. After speaking of the probable origin of the cult, he says—'In our days, indeed, the Druses of Lebanon, in their secret vespers, offer a true worship to the sexual parts of the female, and pay their devotions every Friday night— that is to say, the day which is consecrated to Venus; the day in which, on his side, the Mussulman finds in the code of Mahomet, the double obligation to go to the mosque and to perform the conjugal duty.'"*

"In 1492, Bede mentions that 'a God Krodo is wor- shipped in the Hartz, having his feet on a fish, a wheel in one hand and a pail of water in the other—clearly a Vishnoo or Fishnoo solar deity carrying the solar or lunar disk, and the ark or womb of fertility. These fish-gods, as Mr. Baring Gould states in the case of the American Kox-Kox or Teokipaktli, i.e., fish-god, much resemble the Old Testa- ment Noah, for Kox, encountered a flood and rescued him- self in a cypress trunk (a true phallic symbol), and peopled the world with wise and intelligent beings.' His full title mixes him up with the 'flesh-god' idea of Hebrews and others. North American Indians relate that they too followed

* Ancient Faiths, vol. i.

a fish-man or demi-god from Asia; he was only a man
from the breasts upward, below he was a fish, or, indeed,
two fish, for each leg was a separate fish."*

"It is said Oanes was a man-headed fish, and the
earliest Hermes or Messenger of God to Kaldia. Berosus
says he ate not, yet taught all the arts of geometry, and
the harvesting and storing of fruits and seeds. Every night
he retired to the sea (the Female and Holy Spirit), and
after him came Messiahs. Helladius called him Oes, but
says he had the feet of a man, and sprang from a mundane
egg. He had a fish's skin, and Higgins says he first taught
astrology in Kaldia. The mother of Oanes was worshipped
as Venus Atergates, 'the good spirit,' and Oanes himself
possibly signifies the 'first-born of the Yoni,' the Protogonos
of Sankuniathon. The Japanese represent their Messiah
emerging like Vishnoo from a fish, and as such call him
Kan-On or Can-on, and his temple, Onius, and make his
spirit repose on twelve cushions, just as they do in the
case of Fo or Boodha, showing clearly the solar significance
of the whole. So we see a close connection between the
Kaldian O-AN or Oanes the Hebrew AON, which in Koptic
is the 'Enlightener,' and the Egyptian ON. In Armorik,
Oan and Oanic, and in Irish, UAN is a lamb, and in
Hebrew Jonas signifies the gentle one, a 'Revealer' or
word from God, and a dove, so that the sum of the whole
points to the Sanscrit Yoni.

"Pan, Jove's senior brother, used to be called 'a whale-
like fish,' and he entangled Typhon in his nets and caught
him, and yet who so unlike a fish in character as the
goat-footed god.

"So Boodha is called Day-Po or Fishpo; Vishnoo appears
in the first Avatar as a fish, for he is Viçoo, Fiçoo or
Fish-oo, as Christ is *Ischa* in Ireland, which is the Welsh
Fischa. In all lands, fish have proved the saviours of many
men, and among the fish, the dolphin, as the delphus or
womb. She who has dedicated her life to her God we call
a nun, and this with Hebrews is a fish, and the Yoni.
Fish and birds were called in Asyrian Nanu-Itsurn, yet a
fish spoken of in opposition to a bird was *Kha* and a bird
Khu. Isis was a brooding bird, yet is generally seen with

* Rivers of Life.

a fish on her head. The fish was the first to swallow up the genitals of Osiris, when Typhon caused him to be cut up into pieces and thrown away.

"Eating fish was considered to induce venery even more than beef or garlic, and Shemitic races recommended or ordered such repasts on Frig's Day, or night—their Sabbath or Sabbath Eve. Among the Druses of Syria, Layard assures us such matters are still carefully attended to on Venus' or Frig's Eve, adding that 'in secret vespers' these pious persons 'offer a true worship to the sexual parts of the female.'" *

"Oannes and Dag-on (the fish On) are identical. According to an ancient fable preserved by Berosus, a creature half man and half fish came out of that part of the Erythræan Sea, which borders upon Babylonia, where he taught men the arts of life, to construct cities, to found temples, to compile laws, and, in short, instructed them in all things that tend to soften manners and humanize their lives; and, he adds, that a representative of this animal Oannes was preserved in his day. A figure of him sporting in the waves, and apparently blessing a fleet of vessels, was discovered in a marine piece of sculpture by M. Botta, in the excavations of Khorsabad.

"At Nimroud, a gigantic image was found by Mr. Layard, representing him with the fish's head as a cap and the body of the fish depending over his shoulders, his legs those of a man, his left hand holding a richly decorated bag, and his right hand upraised as if in the act of presenting the mystic Assyrian fir-cone." *(Baring Gould's Myths of the Middle Ages.)*

Mr. Layard, in his interesting work "Nineveh and its Remains," thus alludes to this—"I must not omit to allude to the tradition preserved by Berosus, which appears to attribute to a foreign nation, arriving by sea, the introduction at some remote period of civilization and certain arts into Babylonia. According to the historian, there appeared out of the Erythræan or Persian Gulf, an animal endowed with reason, called Oannes. Its body was like that of a fish; but under the head of the fish was that of a man, and added to its tail were women's feet. Its voice, too, was

* Riv. Life, Forlong.

human, and it spoke an articulate language. During the day it instructed the Chaldæans in letters and in all arts and sciences, teaching them to build temples; but at night it plunged again into the sea. Five such monsters appeared at different epochs in Babylonia, and were called 'Annedoti' (coming out of, or proceeding from). The first was named the Musarus Oannes, and the last Odacon. Their images, he adds, were preserved in Chaldæa even to this day. (This fragment of Berosus is preserved by Apollodorus. See Cory's Fragments.)

'In a bas-relief from Korsabad representing a naval engagement, or the seige of a city on the sea coast, we have the god nearly as described by Berosus. To the body of a man as far as the waist, is joined the tail of a fish. The three-horned cap, surmounted by the flower in the form of a fleur-de-lis, as worn by the winged figures of the bas-reliefs, marks the sacred character. The right hand is raised as in the representations of the winged deity in the circle. This figure is in the sea amongst fish and marine animals. On Assyrian cylinders and germs the same symbolical figure is very frequently found, even more closely resembling in its form the description of Berosus, numerous instances of which are given in Lajard's large work on the Worship of Venus.

"This Fish Worship extended to Syria, and appears to have been more prevalent in that country than in Assyria. The Dagon of the Philistines of Ashdad evidently resembled the figure on the Assyrian sculptures and cylinders. When it fell before the ark, the head and both the palms of his hands were cut off upon the threshold; only the fishy part of Dagon was left to him. (I. Samuel, v. 4; see the marginal reading.) The same idol is mentioned in Judges xvi. The meaning of the word in Hebrew is 'a fish." Although the image, like that of the Assyrians, appears to have been originally male; at a later period, it became female in Syria, as we learn from Lucian (de Deâ Syriâ), and Diodorus Siculus, who describes the idol at Ascalon with the face of a woman and body of a fish. (Lib. ii.) An icthyolatry, connected with Derceto or Atergates, was perhaps confounded with the worship of Dagon." *

"In Azotus, or Asdotus, a renowned city of the Philistines, there was a celebrated temple of Dagon in which the inhabitants kept the ark of the covenant, in presence of the idols. And when they arose early in the morning, behold Dagon was fallen upon his face to the ground before the ark of the Lord, and the head of Dagon and both the palms of his hands were cut off upon the threshold; and rah dagon nischar aghlaju, that is, as R. D. Cimchi explains it, only the form of a fish was left to him. (I. Samuel, v. 4.) For Dag and Dagah are words interpreted to mean fish, whence he was called Dagon. The sacred scriptures, in Hebrews, bestow on him the masculine gender, and so do the authors of the Greek version. Philo Biblius says of Dagon, that he is a fruiterer and the son of Cœlus, and thus thinks he should be called, because he first discovered fruit. For Dagon in Hebrew is translated by the Greek word Siton, which means fruit. He is also said to be the inventor of the plough, therefore was named Zeus the plougher, as if he were Jupiter, the president of agriculture.

"Ptolemus says that Ceres was called Sito among the Syracusans, from the same Greek word Sito. But he is mistaken; for, while he derives it from Dagon (which means fruit), he should have deduced it from Dag (which means a fish). There is the most ancient testimony outside of the Bible in regard to this god of Asia in what Berosus, Apollodorus, and Polyhistor write concerning Oannes. For Oannes is mentioned as a two-headed animal; that feet like those of human beings grew from his tail, and that the rest of him is a fish. His voice was likewise human, and they say that, emerging from the Red Sea, he came to Babylon, but that he returned to the sea at sunset. He did this every day as if he were an amphibious animal, From him men learned all the various arts, letters, agriculture, the consecration of temples, architecture, political government, and whatever could possibly pertain to civilised life, and the most wonderful history of Belus and Omorea. His image was preserved down to the time of Berosus, that is, to the beginning of the Grecian monarchy. This marine god can be no other than Dagon, whose history is found in Samuel. He was worshipped not only by the Philistines, but by the Babylonians also. Apollodorus, from the same Berosus, narrates more extensively of four Oannes, called Annedotos, who likewise in the lapse of ages appeared out of the Red Sea, every one of whom was half man and half fish. But in the time of Ædoracus, king of the Chaldeans, who preceded the deluge a few ages, another similar figure appeared, who was called Odakon. Dagon is undoubtedly intended and referred to in this fable of Odakon. Abydenos speaks of a second Annedotos, and bestows on him the form of a semi-demon. Helladius Besantinus speaks of a certain man of the name of Oleus arising out of the Red Sea, whose head, hands and feet were human, but that the other members of the body were those of a fish and that he taught letters, and the science of astronomy. As all these references are so applicable to the Oannes of Besorus, it is more than probable that the librarian made the mistake in the name of abbreviation in the copy.

"What has been extracted from the Scriptures and what has been said from the writings of the ancients will convince any one that the figure of Dagon was a mixture of the human and marine form. His body was marine, and his face, hands, and feet were human.

"The Scriptures say expressly that his hands and feet were cut off, or broken, when he fell before the ark of the Testament. These ancients wrote that his feet grew to his tail. The Scriptures make him a masculine god, but what has been said elsewhere of the common sex of the gods should be here considered, for this very Dagon was changed into the goddess Adirdaga, that is, Atergatis, Adargatis, Derceto, and those other names mispronounced by the Europeans. It is certain that the Phœnician and Babylon goddess is the very same figure as Dagon, if you will change the sex. Lucianus describes briefly the image of Derceto as seen by him in Phœnicia, and it answers to that of Dagon. But also among other great writers the goddess of Hierapolis is called Derceto, or Atergatis.

"Macrobius contends that, with the figures of Atergatis, she is Astarte, that very mother of gods, and he does not speak of her as any other than that goddess of Hierapolis.

"Unless she had been half fish, she would by no means have been called Derceto. But Atergatis, Adergatis, Atargata, Derceto, Derce, Adargidis, Atargatis, all of which are names of this goddess, are corrupt words, and from Adardaga, which in Hebrew means a magnificent or potent fish. This name was surely most suitable for Oannes, who is said to have conferred so many benefits on mankind.

"In the same way the Sepharvites called their god Adramelech, which means a magnificent king. In the fables there is generally no other reason for the figure than that because formerly Dirce, the daughter of Venus, having fallen into the sea, was by fish preserved from all injuries of the waters, or on account of the metamorphosis of Venus into a fish, when she was running away terrified at the horrible advances of the monstre Typhon.

"Manilius, in his Astronomicon, book fourth, says :—

'When Heaven grew weak and a successful fight,
The gaints raised and gods were saved by flight,
From snaky Typhon's arms, a fish's shape
Saved Venus and secured her from a rape.
Euphrates hid her, and from thence his streams
Owe all obedience to the fish's beams.'

"Or because a fish carried from the Euphrates an egg of wonderful size, which a dove kept warm, and hatched the Syrian goddess; hence it was that they abstained from the eating of fish. They feared that if they ate those animals the vengeance of the goddess would be aroused: that the limbs of their body would swell; that they would be covered by ulcers, and consumed by wasting disease. Plutarch says of the Pythagoreans, that of sea creatures they especially abstained from eating the fish called mullet and urtic. They abstained from eating any kind of fish in order to instruct men and accustom themselves to acts of justice, for they say that fish neither do nor are capable of doing us harm. Others abstained from fish, the same author says, because man arose from a liquid substance, and therefore they worship fish as of the same production and breeding with themselves.

"Anaximander says that men were first produced in fish, and when they were grown up and able to help themselves were thrown out, and so lived upon the land. So he contends that fishes were our common parents.

"Xenophon, in his Anabasis, speaking of the river Chalos, says it was filled with large and gentle fish, which the Syrians worshipped as gods. Neither would they permit them to be injured.

c

"These stories about fish are by no means the growth of the more ancient ages, for about the time of the return of the Israelites from Egyptian bondage, the Tyrians were in the habit of taking fish to Jerusalem for sale. In Nehemiah xiii., v. 16 the words are as follows: 'There dwell men of Tyre also therein, which brought fish, and all manner of ware and sold on the sabbath, unto the children of Judah, and in Jerusalem.' At this time the Jews were not free from the profane rites of their neighbours, particularly such as had taken their wives from among the Philistines, who especially worshipped Dagon. To eat fish or to sell them on the public market-place was surely a great indignity to the god. There were certain fish sacred among other nations, as Pompilius among the Grecians, Anguilla among the Egyptians, and others among the Pythagoreans. In the same way as fish, so were also doves held in great honour out of favour to this god. It is, however, well known that doves were sacred to Venus, and she is Derceto.

"The temple of Dagon is called Beth-Dagon, which is pure Hebrew. (See I. Maccabeus x., 23.) 'The horsemen also being scattered in the field, fled to Azotus and went into Beth-Dagon, their idol's temple, for safety.' Venus of the Ascalonites—that is Derceto—has the very same name with Herodotus, as Mylitta, Alitta, and the mother of the gods, and about the temple of the goddess of Hierapolis fish and doves were received as sacred, and in her honour, no less than where Derceto was worshipped.

"'Paradise Lost' has the following of this deity :—

'Next came one
Who mourned in earnest, when the captive ark
Maimed his brute image, heads and hands lopped off
In his own temple on the grunsel edge,
Where he fell flat, and shamed his worshippers ;
Dagon his name, sea-monster, upward man
And downward fish : yet had his temple high
Reared in Azotus, dreaded through the coast
Of Palestine, in Gath and Ascalon,
And Accaron and Gaza's frontier bounds." *

"Phin.—The old Irish demi-god Pin or Fin seems to have been a form of Pincus, and, like him, was a son of Hermes, sharing, with the Budh or Da-Beoc, the exalted

* Selden's Syrian Deities.

title of Bar-en-di, Son of the One God. It was Fin who conquered the dragon or put down serpent worship and established all the holy rites connected with Crones or Lingams, and, strangely enough, Phins or Feni, as Dr. P. W. Joyce calls them, showed like Eastern Boodhists, a great liking for both charms, which are but small phali, suitable for carrying or wearing on the person. They are exactly like the little Lingas worn on the arms, or secreted on the head or chest of Indian Sivaites. Irish history relates that Christian Feni diligently searched out and revered the teeth of St. Patrick.

"In the Brehon Laws of the Senchus Mor, the Feni or Fiannas, or champions, are described as a real historical people and the lawgivers of Irene. What Arthur and his knights were to Brythonick, British, or 'Little Briton' Kelts, Fin and his Fenians were in the two Skotias or among the Skoti.

"Before the Pagan Phin was converted, he is described as presiding over the Tara assembly 'as a Druid in strangely flowered garments' (note the likeness to Indra and Herakles), and with a double-pointed head-dress, and bearing in his hand a book, like Brahma, Matthew, Vishnoo, and the fishy deities of Assyria, and of the Clonfest Cathedral, County Galway, pictures of which are given by Keane.

"The two-headed mitre of fishy form, the upright rod, spotted or chequered garment, and basket in hand, distinctly mark the Eastern idea of a great Phalik chief, whilst in the mermaid with open book and jaunty arm akimbo, who allows not even the waters to obscure her sexual capacities, we see the Irish idea of Atargatis or Derketis, or 'Divine Ketis,' that form of Venus which Juno assumed at Kupros, in the old Kelto-Pelasgian temple of Kupreuses. There, says Bryant, she was worshipped by the *Pigalia, Pialia* or *Pials*, that is, the worshippers of the Oracle or Pi, who may be called the Pi-i, Phin-i, Pi-ni or Pini, a word which is possibly the base of the Latin and French terms for the Phallus, and which is otherwise of unknown but significant derivation. Macrobius calls *Der-Ketis* 'the mother of the gods,' and Syrians, 'the receptacle of the gods,' that is, an *Erk* or Ark, which the fish represented. If we were fully cognisant of the origin of *Der-Ketis*, it might turn out to be, like the Indian names, a dual or

Linga-in Yoni. Thus Brahma, sitting on the lotus, is called *Brahma-Yoni*, and if *Der* be the Jovine tree or Oak, Der-Ketis would be simply the bi-sexual name of a supreme god. The mythical Semiramis was a daughter of *Der-ketis*, who was changed into a dove, and her mother into a fish, showing the close intertwining of all these figures by phallists." *

"Christians were very partial to the fish, but indeed, may be said to have carried on freely all the ancient ideas, as which faith has not after its first attempt at purification? On Christian tombs especially do fish abound, commonly crossed, which reminds us that crossed serpents denote their act of intercourse, and in this symbolism the fish would be very natural and usual, because denoting new life in death. Derceto, the half-fish and half-woman of the temple of the Dea Syria at Hira, was, says Lucian, the perfection of woman; she was the mystic Oanes, Athor, and Venus, whom Egyptians have handed down to us embalmed.

"So the Fathers of the Church have called their flocks Pisciculi, and their high-priest a fisherman; and have given to all cardinals and bishops the fish-head of Dagon.

"The fish is universally worshipped in all lands as the most fecundative of all creatures; and where most valued, the superstitious have offered it in sacrifice to their gods refusing to eat it. Many a time have I travelled through a poor and barren country where it was all mankind could do to live, and seen rivers and lakes teeming with fine fish which I dared not touch, or only so by stealth as night came on, much to the annoyance of my followers and myself, and the detriment of the people.

"We find Phœnicians, Kelts and Syrians specially mentioned as holding the fish in the greatest reverence, and at different periods of their history not eating it. The hill-tribes towards the sources of the Indus have the same ideas. The Phœnicians picture Dagon and Dorketa the gods of *Gaza* and *As-Kal-on*, as Fish Gods, or perhaps we should say a fish god and goddess, for we know they were also Astartian Deities. *Kuthera* and *Kupros* (Cypress) as shrines of Aphrodite, vied in the worship of this fruitful Kubele, and Syria held the great northern shrine of Hieropolis most

* Forlong.

holy to Venus as the *Fish Goddess*. *Cadiz*, Kodes, or *Gadir-Gades*, had Herkales on one side of her coins, and a fish or Lunette on the other; whilst Syracuse, or rather Soora-Koos, and Soosa alike held their finny multitudes sacred to Fertility. In these days we can imagine what a curse these faiths here were to the poor, and, indeed, to humanity."*

"The high round hill of Tabor, known to Christians as the 'Mount of Transfiguration,' is called by the Fälähin the *umbilicus* of their great earth mother Terra—that womb of nature in which we are transfigured. To her also they had sacred temples at Askalon and Akcho with suitable holy waters; and still at Tripolis, her very ancient city, do we find her pond of holy fish, which are said to 'fight against infidels,' and to which multitudes still make long pilgrimages, and worship with offerings and sacrifices. We have often come across similar holy ponds and lakes in India, and been warned off with our unholy rod and line. The Venus of Tripolis was Kadishah or Atergatis; indeed the city is called Kadishah, a name expressive of coarse phallic vices."*

"Dion Cassius says the Caledonians never taste fish, although their lakes and rivers furnish an inexhaustible supply. Two 'holie fishes' in the seventeenth century occupied a well near the church of Kilmore in Argyleshire. They were black—never changed colour—neither increased in number nor in size in the memory of the most aged. The people believed that no others existed anywhere. Mr. Martin, in his 'Western Isles,' describes the ceremonies practised by invalids who came to be cured by the waters of a well at Loch Saint, in the Isle of Skye. They drank the water and then moved round the well deasil (sunwise), and before departing left an offering on the stone. Martin adds that no one would venture to kill any of the fish in Loch Saint, or to cut as much as a twig from an adjacent copse. These customs practised in the end of the seventeenth century, have apparently reference to the worship of the sun, the fountain, the fish, and the oak.

"The absence of any allusion to the art of catching fish has been used as an argument in support of the

---

* Rivers of Life.

authenticity of the poem of Ossian, as well as being corroborative of the statement of Dion Cassius. Fish-eaters was one of the contemptuous epithets which the Scottish Celt applied to the Saxon and other races that settled in the Lowlands of Scotland, and the remains of the super-stitious veneration of fish, or rather abstaining from fish as an article of food, is registered by the author of 'Caledonia' as influencing the more purely Celtic portions of the British population in the early part of the present century.

"Ancient nations that did not eat but worshipped the fish were the Syrians, Phœnicians, and Celts. But in Caufiristaun, in the remote parts of the Hindu-Cosh, the Caufirs will not eat fish, although it is not said that they worship it. They believe in one great god, but have numerous idols that represent those who were once men and women. A plain stone, about four feet high, represents God, whose shape they say they do not know. One of their tribes call God Dagon. The fish-god and goddess of the Phœnicians were called Dago and Derceto; the worship of Dagon being more particularly celebrated at Gaza and Ashdod; that of Derceto at Ascalon." *

"The old sculptures and gems of Babylon and Assyria furnish sufficient proof of the worship of Fertility, but writers and readers have alike lost the key, or purposely skipped the subject, and this we have a prominent example of in the case of the beautiful Assyrian cylinder, exhibiting the worship of the Fish God, which Mr. Rawlinson gives us without a comment. There we see the mitred man-god with rod and basket adoring the solar Fructifier, hovering over the fruitful tree from which spring thirteen full buds, whilst behind him stands another adoring winged deity backed by a star, a dove, and a yoni. On the opposite side of the Tree of Life is fire, and another man in the act of adoration, probably the Priest of God, pleading with both hands open, that the requests of the other two figures may be granted." †

"I may state that all that the author of Anc. Mons. writes in regard to these old faiths thoroughly supports what I urge, though he is far from looking at their features as I do, for he clearly knows very little of Eastern Phallic

* Leslie's Early Races of Scotland.
† Rivers of Life.

faiths and their interpretation. Ashtoreth is Ishtar or woman, the Star in more senses than one; the Phœnicians call her Astarte, but the 'present Mendean form is Ashtar,' and the plural Ashtaroth. Bunsen derives this representative name from the very coarse, but I fear perfectly correct source, '*the seat of the cow—Has* and *toreth;*' for this is true to the idea of all Hindoos, and shows us that the terms 'male' and 'female' originally meant the *organs pur et simple*, which indeed the writer of Gen. i. 27 expresses in the words *Zakar* and *Nekabah*. In all African and Arabian dialects, *Nana* and not Ishtar is the commonest term for Mother, the usual initial being Ma, Ya, Ye, Ni, and rarely Om and On; see the long list of over one hundred names given by Sir John Lubbock as those of the 'non-Aryan nations of Europe and Asia' and of 'East Africa.' There we see Ma and even *Ama* occasionally used for Father, perhaps because among some tribes the strange custom existed of his going to bed to protect and warm the infant as soon as born. The almost universal initial sounds for the male ancestor are Pa, Fa, Ba, and in a few instances Da and Ad, and once Od and Ta. In Asia Baba, Aba, Apa, and sometimes Ama occur; now what we want to know is the origin of these sounds, but here philology is silent with seemingly no power to advance. This is not the case, however, in regard to the objective roots of religion; here we work with reasoning creatures, and can see that the child continues, and that all mankind have ever continued to mate, whether in their own kind, or in their gods, the same A's, P's, F's, D's, to males, and M's. N's Om's, Y's to females, and we therefore conclude that those were man's earliest symbols and names for the organs of sex, the Omphe or Mamma of the mother, which man had first cognisance of, and the A, Ab or Pa which he noticed as the characteristic of the opposite sex. The Assyrian often represented Ishtar as the upright fish, probably because of the fecundative powers of the fish, and as the creature *par excellence* of water. The great mythic queen Semiramis, wife of Ninus, the founder of Nineveh or Ninus, was said to have sprung from a fish some twenty-three centuries B.C., and to be representative woman, Eva or Mary.

"The mythic genealogy of Semiramis begins with a fish and ends with Ninyas. Her mother was Dorketo the Fish

Goddess of Askalon, in Syria, where she was worshipped as Astarte or Aphrodite. She was famed down to the days of Augustus for her beauty, voluptuousness, virtues and vices. There seems no doubt but that there was some ruler called Semiramis, who conquered most of Western Asia, Egypt and part of Ethiopia, and who attempted India. Her fish origin is simply due to her being a woman and to her marrying *On* or *Ones*, or probably *Oanes* or *Ho-Anes*, the Serpent Fish, or recognised God of Passion, both on the lower Euphrates and the lower Nile. Her conquests may merely signify that the race who had faith in her conquered, or that certain conquerors embraced the worship of the Sun Goddess. When Kaldia fell to Assyria, she was very naturally made to marry Ninus, or the strong Bull-Uan which this name signifies; she was preserved by doves, for these birds were sacred to Aphrodite. Mr. Rawlinson believes that the origin of the myth lies in Ivaloosh's Queen of the eighth century B.C., who was possibly a Babylonian, and shared in the Government with her Lord, but there is little doubt that there was such a queen or goddess. Her name, if embracing Sun and fertilizing energies, would naturally be Sivāmy or Sami (God), Rames, Rami, or Ramesi—the Goddess of the Sun, in fact Ishtar, which Wilford calls her, saying these names mean Isis. The Assyrian story is, that she sprang from a dove or Yoni, which Capotesi would signify, and this is the Indian manifestation."*

* Forlong, Riv. Life.

CHAPTER III

*Universal Love of Flowers—Indifference to Flowers—Excessive
Love of Flowers leading to Adoration—Myths and Legends
connected with Flowers, the Flos Adonis, Narcissus, Myrtle,
Silene inflata, Clover—The Hundred-leaved Rose—The Worship
of the Lily Species—Signification of the Lotos—Hermaphroditic
Character of the Lotos—The Indian Mutiny of 1857, part
played by the Lotos during its Instigation.*

"WHY?" asked a writer some years ago, "why is it that
every eye kindles with delight at the sight of beautiful
flowers? that in all lands, and amidst all nations, the love
of flowers appears to prevail to so great an extent, that
no home is considered complete without them—no festival
duly honoured unless they decorate the place where it is
observed? They are strewn in the path of the bride; they
are laid on the bier of the dead; the merry-maker selects
from the floral tribes the emblem of his joy; and the mourner
the insignia of his grief. Everywhere and under all circumstances, flowers are eagerly sought after and affectionately
cherished; and when the living and growing are not to be
obtained, then is their place filled by some substitute or
other, according to the circumstances or taste of the wearer;
but whether that substitute be a wreath of gorgeous gems
for the brow of royalty, or a bunch of coloured cambric
for the adornment of a servant girl, it is usually wrought
into the form of flowers.

"This taste depends not on wealth or on education, but
is given, if not to all individuals, yet to some of every
class. From the infant's first gleam of intelligence, a flower
will suffice to still its cries; and even in old age the mind
which has not been perverted from its natural instincts, can
find a calm and soothing pleasure in the contemplation of
these gems of creation."

A man, reputed wise, was once asked in a garden:
"do you like flowers?" "No," said he; I seldom find time
to descend to the little things." "This man," said an
American writer, "betrayed a descent, in his speech, to the
pithole of ignorance. Flowers, sweet flowers! he that loves

them not should be classed with the man that hath not
music in his soul, as a dangerous member of the community."

Instead of *not liking* or *not caring*, leaving out, *not
loving* flowers, the general tendency with humanity has been
to run to an opposite extreme and render them not merely
estimation, care or love, but veneration and worship.

The adoration of flowers is one of the most ancient
systems of worship with which we are acquainted. It can
be traced back for ages amongst the Hindus, who believing
that the human soul is a spark or emanation from the Great
Supreme, held that this essence can only be renovated in
man by a communion with his works; it is found amongst
the Chinese, it occupied a most important position in the
mysteries of Egyptain idolatry, it figures prominently on the
past and present monuments of Mexico, and to some extent
prevailed in Europe. Naturally enough, it arose in the
warmer regions of the earth, where the vegetable productions
of the tropics are so much more gorgeous in their colouring
and noble in their growth, and in those regions it still
lingers, after having been swept away in other lands before
the advance of education and a more intellectual religion.

It would be interesting did space allow to enumerate
some of the myths and legends connected with flowers, but
as we have another object in view these must be allowed
to pass with a mere cursory allusion. There is the Flos
Adonis which perpetuates the memory of Venus's favourite,
Adonis, the son of Myrrha, who was herself said to be
turned into a tree called myrrh. Adonis had often been
warned by Venus not to hunt wild beasts; but disregarding
her advice, he was at last killed by a wild boar and was
then changed by his mistress into this flower. There was
Narcissus, too, destroying himself in trying to grasp his
form when reflected in the water by whose margin he was
reclining. Then we have Myrtillus and the Myrtle. The
father of Hippodamia declared that no one should marry
his daughter who could not conquer him in a chariot race;
and one of the lovers of the young lady bribed Myrtillus,
who was an attendant of Œnomaüs, to take out the linch-
pin from his master's chariot, by which means the master
was killed; and Myrtillus, repenting when he saw him dead,
cast himself into the sea, and was afterwards changed by
Mercury into the myrtle.

A bladder campion (Silene inflata) is another curiosity. Ancient writers say that it was formerly a youth named Campion, whom Minerva employed to catch flies for her owls to eat during the day, when their eyes did not serve them to catch food for themselves; but Campion indulging himself with a nap when he ought to have been busy at his task, the angry goddess changed him into this flower, which still retains in its form the bladders in which Campion kept his flies, and droops its head at night when owls fly abroad and have their eyes about them.

The common clover which was much used in ancient Greek festivals, was regarded by the Germans as sacred, chiefly in its four leaved variety. There is indeed, in the vicinity of Altenburg, a superstition that if a farmer takes home with him a handful of clover taken from each of the four corners of his neighbour's field it will go well with his cattle during the whole year; but the normal belief is that the four-leaved clover, on account of its cross form, is endowed with magical virtues. The general form of the superstition is that one who carries it about with him will be successful at play, and will be able to detect the proximity of evil spirits. In Bohemia it is said that if the maiden manages to put it into the shoe of her lover without knowledge when he is going on any journey, he will be sure to return to her faithfully and safely. In the Tyrol the lover puts it under the pillow to dream of the beloved. On Christmas Eve, especially, one who has it may see witches. Plucked with a gloved hand and taken into the house of a lunatic without anyone else perceiving it, it is said to cure madness. In Ireland also it is deemed sacred and has been immortalized in Lover's beautiful song as a safeguard against every imaginable kind of sorrow and misfortune.

It was a belief among the Jews, according to Zoroaster says Howitt, that every flower is appropriated to a particular angel, and that the hundred-leaved rose is consecrated to an archangel of the highest order. The same author relates that the Persian fire-worshippers believe that Abraham was thrown into a furnace by Nimrod, and the flames forthwith turned into a bed of roses.

In contradistinction to this in sentiment is the belief of the Turk, who holds that this lovely flower springs from the perspiration of Mohammed, and, in accordance with this creed, they never tread upon it or suffer one to lie upon the ground.

"Of shrub or flower worship, the most important in the east and south has been that of the lily species. The lily of October—the saffron—was very sacred to the Karnean, or horned Apollo—that is, the sun—for horns usually stand for rays of glory, as in the case of the horned Moses of our poets, artists and ecclesiastics, who make him like an Apis of Egypt, because of the text which says, 'his face shone' when he came down from the mountain. All lilies have more or less to do with the female or fecundating energies, and so even in Europe we have many stories of the crocus species, because it is said 'of their irradiating light, having peculiar looking bells, three-headed and crested capillaments, three cells, and reddish seeds,' &c.

"The Lotus is the seat of most deities, but notably so of the creator Brahma, who, thus enthroned, is called the *Kamāl-a-yoni*, or the great androgynous god. The lotus is the womb of all creation. It is said to originate from the great fertiliser, water, alone; and dropping its great leaves on this fertiliser as on a bed, it springs upwards with a slender, elegant stalk, and spreads forth in a lovely flower. Even the grave and mighty Vishnoo delights in the lotus, which is one of the four emblems he holds in his fourfold arms. It is Venus' sacred flower.

"The flower is shaped like a boat, is a representation of divinity, and is shown as springing from the navel of the great god resting on his milky sea. It always signifies fecundation. Inman, under the head Nabhi, navel, says— 'The germ is "Meroo" (the highest pinnacle of the earth), the petals and filaments are the mountains which encircle Meroo, a type of the Yoni,' and Sanscrit for *mons veneris.* Amongst fourteen kinds of fruit and flowers which must be presented to 'Ananta' (Sanskrit, eternity), the lotus is the only indispensable one, as he (Ananta) is then worshipped in the form of a mighty serpent with seven heads.

"Hindoo and other writers often tell us that the lotus originated the idea of the triangle, which is 'the first of perfect figures, for two lines are an imperfection,' and the lotus also gives us a circle on a triangle which is full of cells and seed, and so is more perfect still. Siva is, as

Orientals know, '*the god of the triangle*,' and hence, in his palace in *Kailasa* we are told the most precious object 'on his table of nine precious stones is the *padma* (lotus), carrying in its bosom the triangle, as origin and source of all things;' and that from 'this triangle issues the Lingam, the eternal god who makes in it his eternal dwelling;' which, however, is not quite correct on the part of M. Guigniant, whom Mr. Barlow quotes. The lotus is an inverted triangle, and is therefore the female sign; the pyramid or triangle on base is Siva, or the *Ray of Light*, the sun-god.

"Another reason why the lotus is in all lands so sacred in its androgynous or hermaphrodite character, a feature imperative in the case of all the great gods of man, though this is not very clear if we dive deeply below the surface, either in the case of the Jewish Elohim or the lotus. Brahma, the creator, whilst sitting on the lotus, as all great gods do, desired, says the 'Hindoo Inspired Word,' to create the universe, and for this purpose, became androgynous, or a breathing-spirit (Ruach?)—prakriti or nature; when creation at once commenced and progressed, much as we have it in the genesis of most faiths. The details of this mystic plant have much exercised all Asiatic and Egyptian minds. In its circular stamina it shows two equilateral triangles placed across each other, which Sanskritists call the *shristi-chakra*, also sixteen petals called the *shoodasa*; and this, it is held, is a revelation from the deity as to the proper age for the representative woman or prakriti, in the Sakti ceremonies. These triangles, with apex upwards and downwards, are *the chapel* or magic diagram which the pious are told to ponder over, for it has many significations and possesses numerous spells; and hence we see it venerated in all early ages, and still an important article of Freemasonry. The spells go by the name of the *devi-chakrams*, or godesses of circles, no doubt having a solar signification.

"The *Padma* and *Kamalata* or *Granter-of-Desires*, or 'Consummator-of-our-Wishes,' are all terms applied to the lotus. It is the symbol of Venus or Lakshmi, or of her incarnation—Krishna's wife, Padha, who is commonly a nude Venus or Sakti. It is also called '*love's creeper*,' the throne and ark of the gods, and the water-born one. One author writes, that from far Thibet to Ceylon, and over every

eastern land and islet, the holy Padma is only a little less
sacred than the Queen of Heaven—Juno (I Oni) herself.
It is as mysterious as the Yoni—is, like it, the flower of
concealment, of night and of silence, and that mysterious-
ness of generation and reproduction; it is described as a
sort of incomprehensible dualism which veils the Almighty
One and his mysteries from our minds.   Linnæus tells us
it is the *Nelumbo*, but R. Payne Knight is clearer when
he writes to this effect.   The flowers of the lotus contain a
seed vessel shaped like an inverted *cone or bell*, which are
very holy symbols with all peoples, and representative male
and female.   This inverted bell is punctuated on the top
with little cavities or cells in which the seeds grow as in
a matrix fed by the parent plant till they arrive at such
a size as to break open 'the ark boat of life.'   They then
emerge and float away, taking root wherever they find
ground, and throwing down long tentacles or tendrills in
quest of it.   The idea is expressed by Brahma in his address
to the angels, as given in the *Linga-Pooran*, beginning:
'When I sprang into existence, I beheld the mighty Narā-
yana reposing on the abyss of waters;' which reminds us
of the Jewish Elohim-god who it is said generated all things
'by brooding o'er the deep.'" *

Those who remember the Indian mutiny of the year
1867 and the long tale of horrors which overwhelmed the
British dominions with grief, dismay and indignation, will
be interested by the information that the conspiracy was
first manifested by the circulation of symbols in the forms
of cakes and lotus flowers.   Commenting upon this, a writer
in "Household Words," of September, 1857, said, after he had
given a description and historical account of the flower: I
fear I may have indulged in too long an excursion into
the realms of botany to suit the reader, who merely wishes
to know why the Indian rebels choose lotus flowers as
symbols of cospiracy.   I am sure I am as innocent of the
knowledge as of the rebellion, but I will try to help my
readers to a guess.   Four-fifths of the human species worship a God-woman; and the vestiges of this worship are
found in the most ancient monuments, documents and
traditions, stretching backwards into the past eternity from

* **Rivers of Life.**

millenium to millenium, towards an epoch beyond the records of the Deluge, and almost coeval with the loss of Eden. The Tentyrian planisphere of the ancient Egyptians represents the virgin and child rising out of a lotus flower. The Egyptian hieroglyphics depict the goddess Asteria, or Justice, issuing out of a lotus, and seating herself upon the centre of the beam of Libra, or the Scales. Pictorial delineations of the judgment of the dead, represent Osiris as Ameuti, swathed in the white garments of the grave, girt with a red girdle, and seated upon a chequered throne of white and black spots, or good and evil. Before him are the vase of nectar, the table of ambrosia, the great serpent, and the lotus of knowledge—the emblems of Paradise. There are Egyptian altar-pieces upon which the lotus figures as the tree of life. The Hindu priests say that the lotus rising out of the lakes is the type of the world issuing out of the ocean of time.

Travellers who have observed the worship of the Hindus and Parsees, tell us that they give religous honours to the lotus. The Budhist priests cultivate it in precious vases, and place it in their temples. The Chinese poets celebrate the sacred bean of India, out of which their god Amida and her child arose, in the middle of a lake. We can be at no loss to imagine the appearance of the Budhist pagodas, for our Gothic cathedrals are just those pagodas imitated in stone. Their pillars copy the trunks of the palm-trees and the effects of the creeping plants of the pagodas; their heaven piercing spires are the golden spathes of palm flowers, and the stained glass reproduces, feebly, the many brilliances of the tropical skies. Every pious Buddist, giving himself up to devout meditations, repeats as often as he can, the words "On ma ni bat mo Klom." When many worshippers are kneeling and repeating the sound, the effect is like counter-bass or the humming of bees; and profound sighs mingle with the repetitions. The Mongolian priests say these words are endowed with mysterious and supernatural powers; they increase the virtues of the faithful; they bring them nearer to divine protection, and they exempt them from the pains of the future life. When the priests are asked to expain the words, they say volumes would be required to tell all their meanings. Klaproth, however, says that the formula is nothing but a corruption of four Hindu

words, " Om man'i padma houm," signifying " Oh ! precious
lotus !" Without pretending that the volume of the Hindu
fakirs on the signification of the lotus, might not throw
more light upon the use of it as a symbol of conspiracy,
there are hints enough in the facts I have stated to
warrant the conclusion that it serves as a sign of a great
and general rising on behalf of Budhism. The flower was
circulated to rally the votaries of the goddess of the lotus.

CHAPTER IV.

*Importance of the Lotos—Varieties of Lotos—Statements by
Herodotus, Homer, Theophrastus, Dioscorides, Pliny, Athenæus
and others—The Aborescent Lotos—The Sacred Lotos of the
Nile—The Indian Lotos—Nepaulese Adoration of the Lotos—
Shing-moo, the Chinese Holy Mother—Lakshmi—The Queens
of Beauty—The Loves of Krishna and Radha.*

THE Lotos is a flower of such importance and prominence
in the subject before us, and especially in connection
with the ancient worship of the East—notably of that of a
phallic character, that we naturally look carefully about us
for the best descriptive information we can find respecting
it. A writer (M. C. Cooke, M.A.) in the "Popular Science
Review" for July, 1871, says:—"The history of sacred
plants is always an interesting and instructive study; more
so when it extends into a remote antiquity, and is associated
with such great and advanced nations as those of Egypt
and India. Much has been written and speculated concerning
the Lotos of old authors; and great confusion has existed
in many minds on account of the desire to make all allusions
and descriptions to harmonise with one ideal plant—the
classic Lotos. We must clearly intimate that it is impossible
to combine all the fragments of history and description
applied to some plant or plants, known by the name of
Lotos—and met with in the pages of Herodotus, Homer,
Theophrastus, and others—into one harmonising whole, and
apply them to a single mythical plant. It is manifest, from
the authors themselves, that more than one Lotos is spoken
of, and it was never intended to convey the notion that,
like immortal Jove, the Lotos was one and indivisible.
Starting, then, with the conviction that the one name has
been applied to more than one or two very distinct and
different plants, we shall have less difficulty than were we
to attempt the futile task of reconciling all remarks about
the Lotos to a single plant."

"In the first instance, it is perfectly clear that the
Lotos of Homer, which Ulysses discovered, and which is
alluded to in the ninth book of the 'Odyssey,' is quite

D

distinct from any of the rest. It is the fruit of this tree
to which interest attaches, and not to the flower as in some
others—this is the arborescent Lotos.

"The second Lotos may be designated as the Sacred
Lotos, or Lotos of the Nile. It is the one which figures
so conspicuously on the monuments, enters so largely into
the decoration, and seems to have been interwoven with
the religious faith of the Ancient Egyptians. This Lotos
is mentioned by Herodotus, Theophrastus, Dioscorides, Pliny,
and Athenæus as an herbaceous plant of aquatic habits, and
from their combined description, it seems evident that some
kind of water-lily is intended. Herodotus says :— 'When the
river is full, and the plains are inundated, there grow in
the water numbers of lilies which the Egyptians call Lotos.'
Theophrastus says :—'The Lotos, so called, grows chiefly in
the plains when the country is inundated. The flower is
white, the petals are narrow, as those of the lily, and
numerous, as of a very double flower. When the sun sets
they cover the seed-vessel, and as soon as the sun rises
the flowers open, and appear above the water ; and this is
repeated until the seed-vessel is ripe and the petals fall off.
It is said that in the Euphrates both the seed-vessel and
the petals sink down into the water from the evening until
midnight to a great depth, so that the hand cannot reach
them ; at daybreak they emerge, and as day comes on they
rise above the water ; at sunrise the flowers open, and when
fully expanded they rise up still higher, and present the
appearance of a very double flower.' Dioscorides says :—
'The Lotos which grows in Egypt, in the water of the
inundated plains, has a stem like that of the Egyptian
bean. The flower is small and white like the lily, which
is said to expand at sunrise, and to close at sunset. It
is also said that the seed-vessel is then entirely hid in the
water, and that at sunrise it emerges again.' Athenæus
states that they grow in the lakes in the neighbourhood of
Alexandria, and blossom in the heat of summer. He also
mentions a rose-coloured and a blue variety. 'I know that
in that fine city they have a crown called Antinœan,
made of the plant which is there named Lotos, which plant
grows in the lakes in the heat of summer, and there are
two colours of it ; one of them is the colour of a rose, of
which the Antinœan crown is made ; the other is called
Lotinos, and has a blue flower.'"

After quoting a number of other descriptions from these authors, the writer proceeds :—"From these descriptions it is evident that the Sacred Lotos of the Nile, the Egyptian Lotos of the ancients, was a species of Nymphœa, common in the waters of that river. Plants, and animals also, submit so much to external circumstances, that the lapse of centuries may eradicate them from spots on which they were at one time common. It by no means follows that the same plants will be found flourishing in the Nile now, that were common under the Pharaohs; but, when the French invaded Egypt in 1798, Savigny brought home from the Delta a blue Nymphœa, which was figured in the 'Annales du Museum,' corresponding very closely in habit to the conventional Lotos so common on the Egyptian monuments.

"It seems to be very probable that the Lotos-flower in the hands of the guests at Egyptian banquets, and those presented as offerings to the deities, were fragrant. The manner in which they are held strengthens this probability, as there is no other reason why they should be brought into such close proximity with the nose.

"There is still a third Lotos mentioned by Dioscorides, Theocritus, and Homer, which may be some species of Medicago or of the modern genus Lotos. It is herbaceous, sometimes wild, and sometimes cultivated; but always written about as though constituting herbage, and is on one occasion cropt by the horses of Achilles. We shall not pause to identify this plant, but proceed at once to the last plant it is our design to deal with.

"The Kyamos, or Indian Lotos. This can scarcely claim to be one of the kinds of Lotos mentioned by the ancients, since it is distinctly alluded to by them as the Egyptian bean, or Kyamos. This plant among the Hindus has a sacred character, equal to that of the Lotus among the Egyptians. It was doubtless Asiatic in its origin, but at one time was plentiful in Egypt, whence it has now totally vanished. It is represented on the Egyptian monuments, but far less common than the Sacred Lotos. Some authors declare this to be the veritable 'Sacred Lotos of Egypt,' a title to which it has no claim. Herodotus, after describing the Lotos, adds—'There are likewise other lilies, like roses (and these, too, grew in the Nile) whose fructification is produced in a separate seed-vessel, springing like a sucker from the root, in appearance exactly resembling a wasp's nest and containing a number of esculent seeds, about the size of olive-berries. These are also eaten when tender and dry.

"Theophrastus describing this plant, says:—'It is produced in marshes and in stagnant waters; the length of the stem, at the longest, four cubits, and the thickness of a finger, like the smooth jointless reed. The inner texture of the stem is perforated throughout like a honey-comb, and upon the top of it is a poppy-like seed-vessel, in circumference and appearance like a wasp's nest. In each of the cells there is a bean projecting a little above the surface of the seed-vessel, which usually contains about thirty of these beans or seeds. The flower is twice the size of a poppy, of the colour of a full-blown rose, and elevated above the water; about each flower are produced large leaves of the size of a Thessalian hat, having the same kind of stem as the flower-stem. In each bean when broken may be seen the embryo plant, out of which the leaf grows. So much for the fruit. The root is thicker than the thickest reed, and cellular like the stem; and those who live about the marshes eat it as food, either raw, or boiled, or roasted. These plants are produced spontaneously, but they are cultivated in beds. To make these bean-beds, the beans are sown in the mud, being previously mixed up carefully with chaff, so that they may remain without injury till they take root, after which the plant is safe. The root is strong, and not unlike that of the reed; the stem is also similar, except that it is full of prickles, and therefore the crocodiles, which do not see very well, avoid the plant, for fear of running the prickles into their eyes."

Major Drury observes that the mode of sowing the seeds, is by first enclosing them in balls of clay, and then throwing them into the water. Sir James Smith says that in process of time the receptacle separates from the stalk, and, laden with ripe oval nuts, floats down the water. The nuts vegetating, it becomes a cornucopœia of young sprouting plants, which at length break loose from their confinement, and take root in the mud.

After comparing these and other accounts, the author of the paper urges that there is no room for doubt that this is the plant which was known to the ancients as the Kyamos or Egyptian bean, the Tamara of modern India.

"The beans and flower stalks of this plant abound in spiral tubes, which are extracted with great care by gently breaking the stems and drawing apart the ends; with these filaments are prepared those wicks which are burnt by the Hindoos in the lamps placed before the shrines of their gods. In India, as well as in China and Ceylon, the flowers are held to be specially sacred."

Sir William Jones says:—"The Thibetans embellish their temples and altars with it, and a native of Nepaul made prostration before it on entering my study, where the fine plant and beautiful flowers lay for examination."

"Thunberg affirms that the Japanese regard the plant as pleasing to the gods, the images of their idols being often represented sitting on its large leaves. In China, the Shing-moo or Holy Mother is generally represented with a flower of it in her hand, and few temples are without some representation of the plant.

"According to Chinese mythology, Shing-moo bore a son, while she was a virgin, by eating the seeds of this plant, which lay upon her clothes on the bank of a river where she was bathing. In the course of time she returned to the same place, and was there delivered of a boy. The infant was afterwards found and educated by a poor fisherman, and in process of time became a great man and performed miracles. When Shing-moo is represented standing, she generally holds a flower in her hand; when she is sitting, she is usually placed upon one of its leaves."*

The Lotos (Lotus) is held in the highest veneration in India, inclusive of Thibet and Nepaul. Amongst the Brahmans and enthusiastic Hindoos, no object in nature is looked on with more superstition; and their books abound in mystical allusions to this lovely aquatic. Being esteemed the most beautiful of vegetables, it not unappropriately furnishes a name for the Hindoo queen of beauty, and Kamal or Kamala is a name of Lakshmi: as is Padma or Pedma, another Sanscrit appellation for both. Under the form of Kamala, Lakshmi is usually represented with a Lotos in her hand, and in most pictures and statues of her consort Vishnu, he is furnished with the Pedma, or Lotus

* See Pop. Science Rev., vol. x.

bud, in one of his four hands, as a distinguishing attribute.
Accordingly, as it is represented in different stages of
efflorescence, it varies, in the eyes of mystics, its emblematical
allusions.   As an aquatic, the Lotos is a symbol also of
Vishnu, he being a personification of water or humidity,
and he is often represented seated on it.   Brahma the
creative power, is also sometimes seated on the Lotos, and
is borne on its calyx in the whimsical representation of
the renovation of the world, when this mystical plant issued
out of the navel of Vishnu from the bottom of the sea
where he was reposing on the serpent Lesha.

Lakshmi, as we have just noticed, is the sakti or consort of Vishnu, the preservative power of the deity.   The
extensive sect of Vaishnava, or worshippers of Vishnu,
esteem Lakshmi as mother of the world, and then call her
Ada Maya; and such Vaishnavas as are saktas, that is,
adorers of the supremacy of the female energy, worship her
extensively as the type of the Eternal Being, and endow
her with suitable attributes.   She is represented by the
poets and painters as of perfect beauty.   Hindoo females
are commonly named after her : and there are few in the
long catalogue of their deities whose various names and
functions are so frequently alluded to in conversation and
writing, either on theogony, mythology, poetry or philosophy.
Her terrestrial manifestations have been frequent, and her
origin various.   As Rhemba, the sea born goddess, she arose
out of the fourteen gems from the ocean when churned by
the good and evil beings for the amrita or beverage of
immortality.   She then assumes the character of Venus
Marina, or Aphrodites of the Greeks, who, as Hesiod and
Homer sing, arose from the sea, ascended to Olympus, and
captivated all the gods.   The production of Rhemba, Sri, or
Lakshmi is thus described in the thirty-sixth section of the
first book of Ramayana.   "The gods, the asuras and the
gandharvas, again agitating the sea, after a long time
appeared the great goddess, inhabiting the lotus ; clothed
with superlative beauty, in the first bloom of youth, covered
with ornaments, and bearing every auspicious sign ; adorned
with a crown, with bracelets on her arms, her jetty locks
flowing in ringlets, and her body—which resembled burnished
gold—adorned with ornaments of pearl.   Thus was produced
the goddess Padma or Sri, adored by the whole universe,

Padma by name. She took up her abode in the bosom of
Padma-nabha, even of Heri," that is, of Vishnu, of whom
these are names.   Sri, as this deity is often called, distinguished her more particularly as the goddess of fortune,
the word meaning *prosperity*; but it is not given exclusively
to Lakshmi. Other of her names are derived from the
lotus, which is the emblem of female beauty, and especially
applicable to this goddess. In images and pictures of her,
which are very common in India, Lakshmi is generally
represented as a mere woman; sometimes, however, four-
armed; often holding a kamal or lotus, in an easy and
elegant attitude, and always very handsome. With her lord,
Vishnu, she is frequently seen on the serpent Sesha; he
reposing, she in respectful attendance, while a lotus springing from Vishnu's navel to the surface of the sea (for this
scene is subaqueous) bears in its expanded calyx, Brahma,
the creator of the world, about to perform the work of
renovation. Sometimes she is seated with her lord on
Garuda, or Superva, clearing the air, of which Vishnu is
a personification. In Vishnu's most splendid avatara, or
incarnation of Krishna, she became manifested as Rukmein,
or Radha, the most adored of the amorous deities, and
mother of the god of love; here again corresponding with
our popular Venus, the mother of Cupid. In the avatara
of Rama, Lakshmi was his faithful spouse, in the form of
Sita; in that of Narsingha she was Narsinhi, or Nrisinhi;
when Varaha, Varahi; and as the Sakti of Narayana she
is by her own sectaries called Narayni; and in most of
the many incarnations of Vishnu she appears to have
descended with him, frequently under his own celestial name:
as his consort generally she is called Vaishnavi.

Lakshmi and Bhavani are both considered queens of
beauty, and their characters are said to "melt into each
other." Lakshmi being commonly seen with a Kamal or
Lotos, the emblem of female beauty, in her hand, she is
called Kamala: the word is by some—by Sir W. Jones,
indeed, in his earlier lucubrations on Hindu mythology,
spelled Kemel. In his profound and spirited hymn to
Narayana, which every inquirer into its subject would do
well to consult with attention, that deity, a personification
of the Spirit of Brahme, as "he heavenly pensive on the
Lotus lay," said to Brahma, "Go; bid all the worlds exist!"
and the Lotus is thus apostrophised :—

" Hail, primal blossom ! hail, empyreal gem !
Kemel, or Pedma, or whate'er high name
Delight thee ; say, what four-formed Godhead came,
With graceful stole, and bearing diadem,
Forth from thy verdant stem ?—
Full-gifted Brahma." *

The following extract from the "Loves of Krishna and
Radha" shews the deep poetic sentiment associated with
flowers, and especially with the Lotos. Krishna, afflicted by
the jealous anger of Radha, exclaims—

"Grant me but a sight of thee, O lovely Radhica!
for my passion torments me. I am not the terrible Mahesa :
a garland of water-lilies, with subtile threads, decks my
shoulders—not serpents with twisted folds : the blue petals
of the Lotos glitter on my neck—not the azure gleam of
poison : powdered sandal wood is sprinkled on my limbs—not
pale ashes. O god of love ! mistake me not for Mahadeva ;
wound me not again ; approach me not in anger ; hold not
in thy hand the shaft barbed with an amra flower. My
heart is already pierced by arrows from Radha's eyes, black
and keen as those of an antelope ; yet mine eyes are not
gratified by her presence. Her's are full of shafts ; her
eyebrows are bows, and the tips of her ears · are silken
strings : thus armed by Ananga, the god of desire, she
marches, herself a goddess, to ensure his triumph over the
vanquished remorse. I meditate on her delightful embrace :
on the vanishing glances darted from the fragant Lotos of
her mouth : on her nectar-dropping speech ; on her lips, ruddy
as the berries of the Bimba."

Radha, half pacified, thus tenderly reproaches him—

"Alas ! alas ! Go, Madhava—depart, Kesavi ; speak not
the language of guile : follow her, O Lotus-eyed god—follow
her, who dispels thy care. Look at his eyes, half-opened,
red with waking through the pleasurable night—yet smiling
still with affection for my rival. Thy teeth, O cerulean
youth ! are as azure as thy complexion, from the kisses
which thou hast imprinted on the beautiful eyes of thy
darling, graced with dark blue powder ; and thy limbs,
marked with punctures in love's warfare, exhibit a letter of
conquest, written in polished sapphire with liquid gold.

* Hindu Pantheon.

That broad bosom, stained by the bright Lotos of her foot,
displays a vesture of ruddy leaves over the tree of thy
heart, which trembles within it. The pressure of her lips
on thine wound me to the soul. Ah! how canst thou
assert that we are one, since our sensations differ thus
widely?—Thy soul, O dark-limbed god! shows its blackness
externally; even thy childish heart was malignant, and thou
gavest death to the nurse who would have given thee milk."

Krishna is thus farther described in the same poem—

"His azure breast glittered with pearls of unblemished
lustre, like the full bed of the cerulean Yamuna, interspersed
with curls of white foam. From his graceful waist flowed
a pale yellow robe, which resembled the golden dust of the
water-lily scattered over its blue petals. His passion was
inflamed by the glances of her eyes, which played like a
pair of water birds with azure plumage, that sport near
a full-blown Lotos on a pool, in a season of dew. Bright
earrings, like two suns, displayed, in full expansion, the
flowers of his cheeks and lips, which glistened with the
liquid radiance of smiles. His locks, interwoven with
blossoms, were like a cloud variegated with moonbeams, and
on his forehead shone a circle of odorous oils, extracted
from the sandal of Malaya—like the moon just appearing
on the dusky horizon, while his whole body seemed in a
flame from the blaze of unnumbered gems."

With respect to the mention above of the *blue* Lotos,
Moor notes:—"Written in the north of India; the Lotos in
the southern parts, Bengal and the Dekhan, having only
white and red flowers. Hence the Hindu poets feign that
the Lotus was dyed red by the blood of Siva, that flowed
from the wound made by the arrow of Kama."

And with respect to the expression, "the bright Lotos
of her foot," he says:—"Hindustani women dye the soles
of their feet, and nails, of a bright red. Redha, in her
frenzied jealousy, fancies she sees a print of her rival's foot
on Krishna's breast; observing, perhaps, the indelible im-
pression of the foot of Brighu, received on his breast by
Vishnu."

"The Indians commonly represent the mystery of their
physiological religion by the emblem of a *Nymphæa*, or *Lotos*,
floating like a boat on the boundless ocean; where the

whole plant signifies both the earth and the two principles
of its fecundation : the germ is both *Méru* and the *Linga*;
the *petals* and *filaments* are the mountains which encircle
Méru, and are also a type of the Yoni ; the leaves of the
calyx are the four vast regions to the cardinal points of
Méru, and the leaves of the plant are the *dwipas* or isles
round the land of *Jambu.* Another of their emblems is
called *Argha,* which means a *cup* or *dish,* or any other
vessel, in which *fruit* and *flowers* are offered to the deities,
and which *ought* always to be *shaped like a boat,* though
we now see arghas of many different forms, oval, circular
or square ; and hence it is that Iswara has the title of
Arghanatha, or the lord of the boat-shaped vessel : a rim
round the *argha* represents the mysterious Yoni, and the
navel of Vishnu is commonly denoted by a convexity in
the centre, while the contents of the vessel are symbols of
the *linga.* This *argha,* as a type of the *adhara-sacti,* or
power of conception, excited and vivified by the *linga,* or
Phallus, we cannot but suppose to be one and the same
with the ship Argo, which was built, according to Orpheus,
by Juno and Pallas, and according to Appolonius, by
Pallas and Argus at the instance of Juno : the Yoni, as
it is usually pronounced, nearly resembles the name of the
principal Hetruscan goddess, and the Sanscrit phrase *Arghanatha* Iswara seems accurately rendered by Plutarch, when
he asserts Osiris was commander of the Argo. We cannot
yet affirm that the words phala, or fruit, and phulla, or a
flower, have ever the sense of Phallus ; but fruit and
flowers are the chief oblations in the *argha,* and triphala is
a name sometimes given, especially in the West of India,
to the trifula, or trident of Mahadeva. It can be shown
that the Jupiter Triphylius of the Pauchœan Islands was
no other than Siva holding a triphala, who is represented
also with three eyes to denote a triple energy, as Vishnu
and Prithivi are severally typified by an equilateral triangle,
(which likewise gives an idea of capacity) and conjointly,
when their powers are supposed to be combined, by two
such equal triangles intersecting each other."*

* See Asiat. Res., vol. iii.

CHAPTER V.

Story of the Fire-God and his secret—Growth of Fire-Worship —Fire an essential in Hindu Worship—The Chaldeans—The Persians—The Hebrews—Fire in Hindu Ceremonies—Duties of Hindu Life—The Serpent and Fire—Phallo-Pythic Solar Shrines—Fire and Phallic Worship—Leaping through Fire— Fire-treading in Scotland—Fire-leaping in Russia—The Medes as Fire Worshippers—The Sabines—Fire and the Ancient Christians—The Roman Church and Fire—The Jews—Temple of Vesta—Fire Worship in Ireland—Phallo-Fire Worship of Greeks and Romans.

THE Rev. W. Gill in his "Myths and Songs from the South Pacific" supplies us with a story particularly suitable for notice here, called the "Fire God's Secret." The story tells us that originally fire was unknown to the inhabitants of the world, who of necessity ate raw food. That in the nether-world (Avaiki) lived four mighty ones : Manike, god of fire ; the Sun-god Rā ; Ru, supporter of the heavens ; and lastly, his wife Buataranga, guardian of the road to the invisible world. To Ru Buataranga was born a famous son Māni. At an early age Māni was appointed one of the guardians of this upper world where mortals live. Like the rest of the inhabitants of the world, he subsisted on uncooked food. The mother Buataranga, occasionally visited her son ; but always ate her food apart, out of a basket brought with her from nether-land. One day, when she was asleep, Māni peeped into her basket and discovered cooked food. Upon tasting it he was decidedly of opinion that it was a great improvement upon the raw diet to which he was accustomed. This food came from nether-world ; it was evident that the secret of fire was there. To nether-world, the home of his parents he would descend to gain this knowledge, so that ever after he might enjoy the luxury of cooked food.

The story goes on to say that when Buataranga set out, next day, on her journey to nether-world, Māni followed her, unbeknown to her. He then saw his mother standing

opposite a black rock which she addressed in these words:
"Buataranga, descend thou bodily through this chasm. The
rainbow-like must be obeyed. As two dark clouds parting
at dawn, Open, open up my road to nether-world, ye
fierce ones!"

At these words the rock divided, and Buataranga descended. Māni carefully treasured up these words; and
started off to see the god Tane, the owner of some wonderful pigeons. He begged Tane to lend him one, but as the
one Tane lent him did not please him, he returned it, as
he did also another and a better one. The only bird that
would content him was a certain red pigeon, which was
specially prized by its owner and was made a great pet
of. Tane at first objected to part with the bird and only
did so upon Māni's faithfully promising to restore it uninjured. Off went Māni with the bird to the place where
his mother had descended. Pronouncing the magic words,
the rock opened, and Māni descended. The guardian demons
of the chasm, enraged at finding themselves imposed upon
by a stranger, tried to seize the pigeon, intending to
devour it. They only succeeded in getting possession of the
tail, which the pigeon went on without. (They say that
Māni had transformed himself into a small dragon-fly and
was perched upon the pigeon's back.)

Arrived at nether-land, Māni sought for the home of
his mother, which was the first house he saw. The pigeon
alighted on an oven-house opposite to an open shed where
Buataranga was beating out cloth. She stopped her work
to gaze at the bird, which she guessed to be a visitor
from the upper world as none of the pigeons in the shades
were red. She said to the bird:—"Are you not come from
daylight?" The pigeon nodded assent; "Are you not my
son Māni?" Again the pigeon nodded. At this Buataranga
entered her dwelling and the bird flew to a bread-fruit tree.
Māni resumed his proper form, and went to embrace his
mother, who inquired how he had descended to nether-world
and the object of his visit. Māni answered that he had
come to learn the secret of fire. Buataranga said, "This
secret rests with the fire-god Manike. When I wish to cook
I ask your father Ru to beg a lighted stick from Manike."
Māni inquired where the fire-god lived. His mother pointed

out the direction, and said it was called Are-ava, *house-of-banyan-sticks.* She warned her son to be careful, "for," she said, "the fire is a terrible fellow, and of a very irritable temper."

Māni walked up boldly towards the house of the fire-god. Manike, who happened to be busy cooking an oven of food, stopped at his work and demanded what the stranger wanted. Māni replied, "A fire brand." The fire brand was given. Māni carried it to a stream running past the bread fruit tree and there extinguished it. He now returned to Manike and obtained a second fire brand, which he also extinguished in the stream. The third time a lighted stick was demanded of the fire-god he was beside himself with rage. Raking the ashes of the oven, he gave the daring Māni some of them on a piece of dry wood. These live coals were thrown into the stream as the former lighted sticks had been.

Māni correctly thought that a fire brand would be of little use unless he could obtain the secret of fire. The brand would eventually go out; *but how to reproduce the fire?* His object therefore was to pick a quarrel with the fire-god, and compel him by sheer violence to yield up the invaluable secret, as yet known to none but himself. On the other hand, the fire-god, confident in his own prodigious strength, resolved to destroy this insolent intruder into his secret. Māni for the fourth time demanded fire of the enraged god. Manike ordered him away, under pain of being tossed into the air; for Māni was small of stature. But the visitor said he should enjoy nothing better than a trial of strength with the fire-god. Manike entered his dwelling to put on his war-girdle; but on returning found that Māni had swelled himself to an enormous size. Nothing daunted at this, Manike boldly seized him with both hands and hurled him to the height of a cocoa-nut tree. Māni contrived in falling to make himself so light that he was in no degree hurt by his adventure. Manike, maddened that his adversary should yet breathe, excited his full strength, and next time hurled him far higher than the highest cocoa-nut tree that ever grew. Yet Māni was uninjured by his fall, whilst the fire-god lay panting for breath.

It was now Māni's turn. Seizing the fire-god he threw him up to a dizzy height and caught him again like a ball with his hands. Without allowing Manike to touch the ground, he threw him a second time into the air, and caught him in his hands. Assured that this was but a preparation for a final toss which would seal his fate, the panting and thoroughly exhausted Manike entreated Māni to stop and to spare his life. Whatever he desired should be his.

The fire-god, now in miserable plight, was allowed to breathe awhile. Māni said, "Only on one condition will I spare you—*tell me the secret of fire. Where is it hidden? How is it produced?* Manike gladly promised to tell him all he knew, and led him inside his wonderful dwelling. In one corner there was a quantity of fine cocoa-nut fibre; in another, bundles of fire-yielding sticks—the *au*, the oronga, the tauinu, and particularly the aoa or banyan tree. These sticks were all dry and ready for use. In the middle of the room were two smaller sticks by themselves. One of these the fire-god gave to Māni, desiring him to hold it firmly, while he himself plied the other most vigorously. And thus runs the Fire-god's Song :—

> " Grant, oh grant me thy hidden fire,
>   Thou banyan tree !
> Perform an incantation ;
> Utter a prayer to (the spirit of)
>   The banyan tree !
> Kindle a fire for Manike
> Of the dust of the banyan tree."

By the time the song was completed, Māni, to his great joy, perceived a faint smoke arising out of the fine dust produced by the friction of one stick upon another. As they persevered in their work the smoke increased ; and, favoured with the fire-god's breath, a slight flame arose, when the fine cocoa-nut fibre was called into requisition to catch and increase the flame. Manike now called to his aid the different bundles of sticks and speedily got up a blazing fire, to the astonishment of Māni.

The grand secret of fire was secured. The story tells us that the victor then in order to be revenged for his trouble and his tossing into the air, set fire to his adversary's abode, that in a short time all the nether-world was in flames, which consumed the fire-god and all he possessed.

Māni then picked up the two fire-sticks and hastened to the bread-fruit tree, where the red pigeon awaited his return. His first care was to restore the tail of the bird so as to

avoid the anger of Tane. There was no time to be lost, for
the flames were rapidly spreading. "He re-entered the pigeon,
which carried his fire-stalks one in each claw, and flew to the
lower entrance of the chasm. Once more pronouncing the
words he learnt from Buataranga, the rocks parted, and he
safely got back to this upper world. Māni now resumed his
original human form, and hastened to carry back the pet
bird of Tane. Passing through the main valley of Keia, he
found that the flames had preceded him, and had found an
aperture at Teava, since closed up. The king's Rangi and
Mokoiro trembled for their land; for it seemed as if everything would be destroyed by the devouring flames. To save
Mangaia from utter destruction, they excited themselves to
the utmost, and finally succeeded in putting out the fire.
Rangi thenceforth adopted the new name of Matamea, or
Watery-eyes, to commemorate his sufferings; and Mokoiro was
ever after called Anai, or Smoke."

"The inhabitants of Mangaia availed themselves of the
conflagration to get fire and to cook food. But after a time
the fire went out, and as they were not in possession of the
secret, they could not get new fire.

"But Māni was never without fire in his dwelling; a
circumstance that excited the surprise of all. Many were the
inquiries as to the cause. At length he took compassion on
the inhabitants of the world, and told them the wonderful
secret—that fire lies hidden in the hibiscus, the urtica argenta,
the 'tauinu' and the banyan. This hidden fire might be
elicited by the use of fire sticks which he produced. Finally,
he desired them to chant the fire-god's song, to give efficacy
to the use of the fire-sticks."

"From that memorable day all the dwellers in this upper
world used fire-sticks with success, and enjoyed the luxuries
of light and cooked food.

"To the present time this primitive method of obtaining
fire is still in vogue; cotton, however, being substituted for
fine cocoa-nut fibre as tinder. It was formerly supposed that
only the four kinds of wood found in the fire-god's dwelling
would yield fire.

"'Aoa' means banyan-tree; for intensity and rhythm the
word is lengthed into 'aoaoaoa.' The banyan was sacred to
the fire-god.

"The spot where the flames are said to have burst

through, named Te-oao or *the banyan-tree*, was sacred till Christianity induced the owner to convert the waste land into a couple of taro patches." *

"Light, then fire, the sun, and the 'whole host of heaven' seem successively, and at last collectively, to have become objects of worship to the Arian race; but first of all light, which was to them pre-eminently the object of adoration in Northern India previous to the period of the collection or composition of the hymns of the earliest Hindu Veda, or, in round numbers, thirty-five centuries ago.

"According to Herodotus, the Persians venerated fire as a divinity, and Pliny explains that the magic of Persia might apparently have been learned from the practices of the Britons. There is abundant evidence to show that our heathen ancestors worshipped the sun and moon. It might, therefore, reasonably be inferred that in Britain, as in other countries, fire would be substituted as typical of the great luminary—of its light and its heat—and became an object of adoration, when the sun was obscured or invisible in seasons set apart for celebrating the religious rites of a Sabian worship. But we are not dependent on inference, however rational, for a knowledge of the fact that fire was an object of adoration to our heathen ancestors, even so late as the eleventh century; for in the laws of Cnut fire appears as one of the objects the worship of which is forbidden."

"Fire seems to have always had the firmest hold upon the wonderment and then the adoration of the infant mind. To the present moment it is an essential part of all Hindoo worship and ceremonies. From his cradle to his grave, when the Hindoo is folded in the god's embrace, the ancient races around me seek for it, use it, offer sacrifices to it, and adore it."

The Chaldeans had a high veneration for fire, which they accounted a divinity; and in the province of Babylon there was a city consecrated to this usage, which was called the city of Ur, or of Fire.

The Persians also adored God under the image or representation of fire, because it is fire that gives motion to everything in nature. They had temples which they called

---

* For a somewhat longer account of this and other Myths, see Rev. W. Gill's Book.

"Pyræa," fire temples set apart solely for the preservation of the sacred fire. They are said to have in that empire fires still subsisting which have burnt many thousand years.

The worship of the goddess Vesta and of fire, was brought into Italy by Æneas and the other Trojans who landed there; but the Phrygians themselves had received it from the eastern nations. Fire was held in religious veneration among the Gauls; and similar sentiments and practices have prevailed in several countries of America.

The Hebrews kept up the holy fire in the temple. This holy fire descended from heaven, first upon the altar in the tabernacle at the consecration of Aaron and his sons to the priesthood, and afterwards it descended anew on the altar in the temple of Solomon, at the consecration of that temple. And there it was constantly maintained by the priest day and night, without suffering it ever to go out; and with this all the sacrifices were offered that required fire. This fire, according to some of the Jewish writers, was extinguished in the days of Manasseh; but the more general opinion among them is, that it continued till the destruction of the temple by the Chaldeans; after that it was never more restored; but instead of it, they had only common fire in the second temple.

The part played by fire in the life of a Hindoo is a remarkable one, and shews the immense extent to which this form of worship has prevailed and still prevails in some countries. In the man's earliest days—in his childhood—at the ceremony called the investiture of the thread, fire is kindled from the droppings of the sacred cow, sprinkled with holy water and blessed. Then are brought to it various offerings of grain, butter, &c., by the worshippers who are supplicating blessings, the officiating priest all the while reading passages from the sacred books. The child's father and mother pray to Agni (Fire) that its past sins may be forgiven, having been done in ignorance; then they declare him to be of an age to know good and evil—he is between seven and nine. The sacred thread is then, after being duly washed and held over the fire, placed around the child's neck, constituting him a Brahm Achari—one sworn to practise the laws and behests of Brahm or Almighty God. Dubois, in Mœurs des Indes, says—"A pious father will then say

E

privately to his child, 'Remember, my son, there is but one God, the Sovereign Master and Principle of all things, and every Brahman is bound to worship him in secret.'"

A fortnight afterwards, a kind of confirmation ceremony takes place, again before the fire, in which the parents promise that they will see that he gets married and leads a good life.

Marriage is the principal feature in a Hindoo's life, and this, as most people know, takes place very early and is attended with many important ceremonies.

Here, again, fire is conspicuous as an object of worship, the ceremony before it—the God Agni—being the last and most serious of all.   With clothes tied together, bride and bridegroom parade round about the deity casting to him their offerings which now "symbolise," says Forlong, "the sacrifice of all their virgin modesty to the god, as the emblem of sexual fire."   The final oath of mutual love and faith is then taken in an address to the fire, and the pair, who are mere boy and girl, are duly married.

A little further on when the period arrives for cohabitation, the fourth ceremony is then gone through, fire again being adored and sacrifice offered.

In the final scene, when death has taken possession of the body, fire is again called into requisition; it is carried before the corpse by the nearest relatives, and ultimately reduces the inanimate form to its original dust and ashes.

Forlong says—"Fire enters into every duty of a Hindoo's life.   Before partaking of his morning meal he utters incantations to Agni, offers to him portions of that meal; and in like manner, before he wears a new cloth or garment, he must take some threads or parts of it and offer these to the same deity."

"It is from the rubbing together of the wood of trees, notably of the three Banian figs—Peepal, Bar, and Gooler, the favourite woods for Phallic images, that holy fire is drawn from heaven, and before all these species do women crave their desires from God."

"Cave and fire rites are not yet extirpated from Jeru-salem, nor, indeed, from any nation of the earth.   Christians still rush for sacred fire to the holy cave at the birth of Sol, and men and women strive, in secret nooks, to pass naked through holy fire."

"Syrians, as well as all other nations, connected the Serpent with Fire. Thus the Jews had their fire altars, on which the holy flame must be ever burning and never go out; and they carried about a serpent on a pole as their healer. So also the writer of the Acts of the Apostles speaks of the Christian Holy Ghost as having serpent-like 'cloven tongues of fire,' which the margin of orthodox Bibles very properly connects with Isaiah's Seraphim."

Forlong says:—"I began my study of British ruins about eight years ago (from 1882), during a two-year-furlough, attracted to it at first by my friend the late Sir James Simpson—President of the Society of Antiquaries, Edinburgh —at that time writing and debating much on these matters; and I came then to the same conclusion as I hold to-day; viz.: that the ruins of Armorika, those of Stonehenge, Abury, and various others, known popularly as 'Druid Circles,' are, or originally were, Phallo-Pythic—Solar shrines, or places where all the first five elemental faiths more or less flourished; the first (Tree) very little, and the last (Sun) very abundantly; and if so, then we see the cause why European writers so pugnaciously hold out, some for Sun, some for Fire; one that they are mere places for sacrifices or burial, or for assembly of rulers, clans, &c.; whilst a few outlying writers hint that the large stones are Lingams, or mere groups of such stones as that of Kerloaz—the Newton stone, &c. Colonel Forbes Leslie, in his 'Ancient Races of Scotland,' has very nearly told us the truth, his long residence and travels in Asia having enabled him almost to pierce the cloud, though he seems at first not to have fully appreciated the ever very close connection between Sun, Fire, Serpent and Lingam faiths, which I believe he does now."

"The European mind having once lost the old ideas of what these words meant, and from having still such objects as Sun, Fire, and Serpent before them, is always thinking of these visible objects, which I might almost say a true Sivaite never recognises *per se;* for in fire the true Phallic worshipper sees no flame, and in the sun no far-out resplendent orb as we know, standing apart, as it were, in space, and to which we all gravitate; he sees simply a source of fertility, without which the Serpent has no power or passion, and in whose absence the animal and vegetable world must cease to exist. The fire here, then, is not that

which the real Sivaite sees or cooks by, but Hot or *Holy
Fire*, or the 'Holy Spirit,' or the fire of passion, which to
a certain small extent, and in certain symbolic forms and
positions, he recognises in flame, as when raised on a tower,
coming out of an obelisk, or rising in a column or pillar
over an ark, or smouldering in the secret adytum; for the
first impresses him with the Arkite, the second with the
Phallic and Arkite, and the third with the purely feminine
idea; in all, he merely sees representative male and female
energies which are excited and fructified by the Sun, Apollo,
or the Sun-Serpent, as in his old coin, where fertility fed by
fire feeds the shell. In a column, be it wood, stone, or fire,
he sees the Sun-stone, such as the Mudros of Phœnicia, the
Mindir of Ireland, and obelisk of Egypt; and in the cist,
shell, or Akros, the womb, Yoni, or sun-box; in all, the
column or Palas, and its Caput-oline."

"Leaping or walking through the fire, so frequently
mentioned in Jewish writings in connection with Molek, is
still quite common in the less civilised parts of India, being
usually done in fulfilment of a vow for blessings desired, or
believed to have been conferred by the deity upon the
Nazarite or Vower. I have known of it being gone through
for recovery from a severe illness, and for success in an
expedition or project which the Nazarite had much at heart."

Some say fire should be trod because Drupadi, the
mythical wife of the Pandoos, did this, after defilement
through the touch of Kichaka, and because Sita proved her
purity by fire. Where the British Government can prevent
this rite, flowers are thrown into the fire-pit, which seems as
if the fire were looked upon as a female energy. Fire-treading
is commonly accomplished by digging a deepish narrow pit,
and filling it with firewood, and then when the flames are
scorching hot, leaping over it; usually the rite begins by first
walking closely round the fire, slowly at first, then faster
and faster, with occasional leaps into and out of it in the
wildest excitement. Mr. Stokes, of the Madras Civil Service,
thus describes the rite as it came officially to notice in
April, 1873.

In a level place before the village deity, who was
Drupadi Ama (Mother D.), a fire-pit, in size 27 by $7\frac{1}{2}$ feet
by 9 inches deep, was excavated east and west, and the
goddess set up at the west end. Six Babool or Acacia trees

(this being a fiercely burning wood) were cut and thrown in; thirteen persons trod this fire, and one died from the effects. They followed each other, some with tabors, others ringing a bell, and each, after passing through the fire, went into a pit filled with water, called the "milk pit." All merely wore a waist cloth, and had their bodies daubed over with sandal. The one who died, fell into the fire, and had to be pulled out. The fire was lit at noon, and "walking it" took place at two p.m., when it had become very bright and hot. The Poojore, or priest of the temple, said it was his duty to walk annually through the fire, and that he had done so for seven or eight years. It was the mother of the dead man who had vowed that if her son recovered from an attack of jaundice she would tread the fire, but the old woman being blind, her son fulfilled the vow. Some said that the dead man himself had vowed thus to the Goddess Drupadi: "Mother, if I recover, I shall tread on your fire." Death is rarely the result of this practice, but Mr. Stokes adds that a few years ago, a mother and her infant died from the effects.

"On the 29th of June, men, and even babes, had to be passed through the fire. 'On this night,' says Dr. Moresin, 'did the Highlanders run about on the mountains and high grounds with lighted torches, like the Cicilian women of old, in search of Proserpine,' and Scotch farmers then used to go round their corn-fields with blazing torches, as was the custom at the Cerealia. The ancient Roman Kalendar states, among other matter, that fires are made on the 23rd; 'Boys dress in girls' clothes; waters are swum in during the night. Water is fetched in vessels and hung up for purposes of divination; fern is esteemed by the vulgar because of the seed . . . .; girls gather thistles, and place a hundred crosses by the same;' for has not the thistle a cap like the lotus, and is it not a trefoil?

"In the 'Englishwoman in Russia,' p. 223, a writer says that 'on midsummer eve a custom still (1855) exists in Russia, among the lower classes, that could only be derived from a very remote antiquity, and is perhaps a remnant of the worship of Baal. A party of peasant women and girls assemble in some retired unfrequented spot, and light a large fire, over which they leap in succession. If by chance one of the other sex should be found near the place, or should have seen them in the act of performing the rite, it is at the imminent hazard of his life, for the women would not scruple to sacrifice him for his temerity.' The writer was assured that such instances had often been known. Thus this 'Fire-dance' is a very serious matter, and one which under the circumstances, we can learn very little about: from its secret practice here by women it is clearly connected with Agni, the Procreator or Fertiliser. Our ancestors were inveterate fire-worshippers, especially at the four great solar festivals. They thought no cattle safe unless passed through the May Day and Midsummer Beltine fires, and no person would suffer a fire within their parish which had not been then kindled afresh from the Tin-Egin, or sacred fire produced by friction."

The Medes were undoubtedly worshippers of Fire, "as the most subtle, ethereal, incomprehensible, and powerful agent. They were averse to all temples or personification of the material things, or of Ormazd. Like our Parsee fellow-subjects, they never allowed their hearth-fires to be extinguished, nor would they even blow out any ordinary fire or candle; in the Magian days, he who did so forfeited his life."

"We still see the remains—some very perfect—of the lone Fire-towers, which Greeks called *Puraitheia*, amidst the lofty hills of Armenia, Azerbijan, Koordistan and Looristan, some of which were Dakmas, or 'Towers of Silence,' having gratings for roofs, through which the bones fell when the body was destroyed. The Fire-God was called *At-Ar*."

The Sabines were, perhaps, more nearly related to our ancestors than is generally thought; at least we may believe so from the Sabine and Gælic languages having more affinity even than the Welsh and Irish, and from other evidence. Dr. Leatham, in his work on *Descriptive Ethnology*, says that 'much of the blood of the Romans was Keltic, and so is much of the Latin language,' and a study of the movements of ancient peoples will show how this is so. Like the Skyths, these old Sabines were devoted to all the worship of Sivaites, and particularly of Mars' symbol, the Quiris or Spear, after which we still call their greatest fête Quirinalia, and their Mount Zion, the Quirinal. The worship of the *Quiris* has not yet ceased in high Asia, nor, I believe, in America. It was prominent on the summits of all the Skythian bonfire piles and mounds at which these Aryan fathers worshipped, and is connected with most rites. We also see it on numerous sculpturings which have been un-earthed from the ruins of the Skuti, or Kelts of Ireland and Scotland—much to the perplexity of local antiquaries. Huc, in his 'Travels in Tartary,' gives us these Phalli as existing all over the immense extent of country he traversed, including Northern China, Mongolia, Thibet. Spears are, however, too valuable to be left sticking in 'these *Obos*,' as he calls them, and therefore 'dried branches of trees' are substituted in very good imitation of spears."

"We have abundant proof that Fire was never neglected by ancient Christians, either on tomb or altar. In a letter from Rome, we find that in front of the Cubiculum, or square tomb of Cornelius the martyr, is a short pillar supporting an ever-burning lamp of oil; and when this custom of never-dying flame—alike common to all faiths— was revived in the third century A.C., we read that the Popes used to send to kings and queens a few drops of the oil from this lamp of the tomb of Cornelius. (See Cor.— Ill. Lon. News, 3-72.) Nor need we be astonished at this, seeing that Vesta's shrine still flourished and received Papal attention, and that in every corner of the world Fire-faith existed. To this day none may neglect the rites of this faith in Syria—cradle of the God, as the poor Turkish Bey of Antioch and his son found to their cost, when, after the earthquake of April 3rd, 1872, they and their officers kindly, reverently and wisely buried the Christian dead, but without the fire-symbols and bell-ringing (which they failed to under-stand), thereby greatly offending a powerful sect of Antioch, called the Dusars, who, still clearly worshipping Baal and Astaroth, rose upon the poor Turks and smote them hip and thigh."

"In the county of Kildare, Ireland, 'everlasting fire' was preserved by 'holy virgins—called *Ingheaw Andagha*, or *daughters of fire*,' down to the time of the Reformation. These were often the first ladies of the land, and never other than those of gentle birth."

"No blessing can be asked or granted from the altar of any Catholic Church until the candles are lighted. If a woman when pregnant desires to be blessed by the Christian Church, she is instructed 'to wait on her knees, at the door of the church, with a lighted taper in her hand,' nor can

any cross be blessed until three tapers are lighted by the
'man of God,' had placed at its base.   See Picart II., 117,
where he gives some graphic plates of Christian Phallo-
solar-fire rites.

"In Goodwin's *Civil and Ecclesiastical Rites*, under the
head of *Feasts of the Expiation*, which we have reason to
believe was at one time a period of human sacrifice, we
have the great Winter-Christmas Saturnalia, or Juvenalia
Festival of Lights and Fires described, when not only the
temples of Jews and Christians, but every house had to be
carefully lighted.   Jews taught that the lights must be held
in the left hand, and the holder must 'walk between two
commandments,' which seems to denote the climatic or solar
turn of the year.   This old writer tells us that it was
'woman's peculiar province to light their lamps;' and that
'there are certain prayers appropriated to this festival, and
among the rest *one in praise of God, who hath ordained
the lighting up of lamps upon Solemn Days.*'   Here we see
a close resemblance between the faith of the Jew and the
Islami, whose wives are enjoined personally to see to the
lighting of the household lamps on Venus' Eve.   Jerusalem,
we know, acknowledges the God of Agni to the present
hour, by annually giving out that holy Fire descends from
heaven at a stated season into the dark Adyta of the
Sacred Shrine; all old fires must be extinguished at this
the season of Sol's renewed vigour, so when the priest
emerges from the adytum with the new fire in his hand
(and Christian priests have often done this, if they do not
do so still), crowds of every hue and creed rush towards
him, light their tapers, and bear away the new fire to their
homes."

Referring to the Temple of Vesta mentioned by Davies,
Forlong says—"Now, what was this Temple of Vesta?   In
its rites and surroundings, its duties social and political,
it was one with the temples still existing in Asia devoted
to Phallic and Fire-worship combined, or perhaps I should
say a temple to Phallic worship only, but the cult in the
dawn of brighter faiths was somewhat hid away by the
priests in the darkest recesses of their temples, and not
well-known by many of the worshippers, and scarcely at all
by European writers even of the middle ages.   Any student
of Delphic lore and of Eastern travel, however, will recognise

at once in Delphi's Oracle and Vesta's Temple, 'The Old Faith' and its priestess worshippers, although the writer in Smith's Dictionary of Antiquities does not appear to do so. He describes Vesta's as merely a Fire-temple, and says that there were six Vestales or Virgin Priestesses to watch the eternal Fire which blazed everlastingly on the altar of the goddess. On the Pope has descended the name of their superior as 'Pontifex Maximus.' If by any negligence or misfortune the Fire went out, the Pontifex Maximus scourged the erring vestal virgin, for had not she—a woman—permitted the procreative energy of the god to forsake mankind?"

"Dr. George Petrie, who in 1845 still combatted, but without force, the pre-Christian idea of Irish Towers, acknowledges signs of a very strong and all-prevailing Fire Worship in Ireland. This he sees in Bel or Bil-tene— 'the goodly fire,' in which Bel, the sun in Ireland, as of old in Babylon, was the great purifier. The Druids, he says, used to worship in presence of two fires, and make cattle walk between them to keep off evil. Even in Dublin we have still May-fires, and those of St. John's Eve; and an old manuscript of Trinity College tells us that 'Bel was the name of an idol at whose festival (Bel-tine) a couple of all cattle were exhibited as in his possession,' which I conclude means—fixed by his rays. The name of this feast in Scotland was Egin-Tin, in which we can recognise Agin, Ag, or Agni-fire, and the fire-god of all Asia. In the island of Skye—says Dr. Martin, quoted by Petrie, page xxxviii.—the Tin Egin was a forced fire or fire of necessity which cured the plague and murrain amongst cattle. All the fires in the parish were extinguished, and eighty-one married men (a multiple of the mystic number nine) being thought the necessary number for effecting this design· took two great planks of wood, and nine of them were employed by turns, who, by their repeated efforts, rubbed one of the planks against the other until the heat thereof produced fire, and from this forced fire each family is supplied with new fire.

"This is the true 'fire which falls from heaven,' and it must still be so produced at the temples of all fire-worshipping races, and at the hearths of the Guebre or Parsees, as it was in this remote Isle of Skye.

"I must now make a few general observations upon

the marked Phallo-Fire Worship of the Greeks and Romans, too commonly called 'Fire and Ancestor Worship,' it not being perceived that the ancestor came to be honoured and worshipped only as the *Generator*, and so also the Serpent, as his symbol.

"The 'Signs' or Nishans of the generating parents, that is the Lares and Penates, were placed in the family niches close to the holy flame—that 'hot air,' 'holy spirit,' or "breath'—the active force of the Hebrew BRA, and the Egyptian P'ta—the engenderer of the heavens and earth, before which ignorant and superstitious races prayed and prostrated themselves, just as they do to-day before very similar symbols.

"The Greeks and Romans watched over their fires as do our Parsees or Zoroastrians. The males of the family had to see that the holy flame never went out, but in the absence of the head, and practically at all times, this sacred duty devolved on the matron of the house. Every evening the sacred fire was carefully covered with ashes so that it might not go out by oversight, but quietly smoulder on; and in the early morning the ashes were removed, when it was brightened up and worshipped. In March or early spring it was allowed to die out, but not before the New Year's Fire had been kindled from Sol's rays and placed in the sanctuary. No unclean object was allowed to come near Agni; none durst even warm themselves near him; nor could any blameworthy action take place in his presence. He was only approached for adoration or prayer; not as fire, which he was not, but as *sexual flame* or *life*. Prayers were offered to him similar to those Christians use; and with most he held just such a mediatorial office as Christ does. The Almighty was addressed through him, and he was asked for health, happiness wisdom and foresight; guidance in prosperity and comfort in adversity, long life, off-spring, and all manly and womanly qualifications. His followers were taught that it was the most heinous sin to approach him with unclean hearts or hands, and were encouraged to come to him at all times for repentance and sanctification.

"Before leaving the house, prayer had to be made to the sacred fire; and on returning, the father must do so

even before embracing his wife and children. Thus Agamemnon acted, we are told, on his return from Troy. Sacrifices,
libations, wine, oil and victims were regularly offered to the
Fire, and as the god brightened up under the oils, all
exulted and fell down before him. They believed that he
ate and drank, and with more reason than the Jew said
this of his Jehovah and El-Shadai. Above all, it was
necessary to offer food and wine to him; to ask a blessing
before every meal, and return thanks when it was over.
From Ovid and Horace we see it was thought pious and
proper to sup in presence of the sacred flame, and to make
oblations to it. There was no difference between Romans,
Greeks, and Hindoos in these respects, except that Soma
wine in India took the place of the grape of cooler lands.
All alike besought Agni by fervent prayers for increase of
flocks and families, for happy lives and serene old age, for
wisdom and pardon of sin. We see the great antiquity of
this faith in the well-known fact, that even when the early
Greeks were sacrificing to Zeus and Athene at Olympia,
they always first invoked Agni, precisely as had been ordered
in the Vedas some 2,000 years B.C., and probably as he
had been invoked many thousands of years before the art
of writing was known."

CHAPTER VI.

Fire-worship in the States of the Mediterranean—Special Sacredness of the public City-fire of Greece and Rome—The sacred Fire of Tlachtga—Ceylon Fire-worship—The Parsees—Persian Monuments—Impiety of Cambyses—Cingalese Terms, Sanscrit, Welsh, &c.—The Yule-log—Fire-worship in England—The Fire of Beltane—Druidical Fires—May-day Fires—November Fires in Ireland—Between Two Fires—Scotland—The Summer Solstice and Fire Ceremonies—Worship of Baal in Ireland—St. John's Day—Bonfires—Decree of Council of Constantinople.

"ALL the states of the Mediterranean and Persia had, like India, baptismal forms connected with Fire. With the Greeks and Romans the baptismal ceremony took place between the ninth and twelfth days of birth, and generally commenced by women seizing the infant and running round, or dashing through the fire with it. So also at marriages, fire was the active and 'covenant god.' No account was taken of a brides faith; to marry was to embrace the husband's religion, to be to him *in filiæ loco*, and to break entirely with her own family; nay, marriage was for long entered into with a show of violence, as if to demonstrate the separation. It certainly reminds one of early times when men thus obtained their wives. The principal part of the marriage ceremony was to bring the bride before her husband's hearth, anoint her with holy water, and make her touch the sacred fire; after which she broke bread or ate a cake with him. Fire was also the God who witnessed the separation of husband and wife, which, if there were offspring, was a rare and difficult act; but if the couple were childless, divorce was an easy matter."

"No stranger dared appear before the city-fire either in Greece or Rome, indeed the *mere look* of a person foreign to the worship would profane a sacred act, and disturb the auspices. The very name of strangers was *hostis*, or enemy to the gods. When the Roman Pontiff had to sacrifice out-of-doors, he veiled his face so that the chance sight of strangers might be thus atoned for to the gods, who were supposed to dislike foreigners so much, that the most laborious ceremonies were undertaken if any of these passed near, not to say handled any holy object. Every sacred fire had to be re-lit if a stranger entered a temple; and so in India, every sacred place must be carefully purified if a foreigner (ruler and highly respected though he may be) pass too close to a Hindoo shrine. I have seen Government servants under me, and Sepoys, who meant no disrespect, throw away the whole of a day's food, and dig up the little fire-places they had prepared before cooking and eating, because, by accident or oversight, my shadow had passed over it; though sometimes, if there were no onlookers, this extreme measure was not carried out, partly out of regard for me."

Dr. Keating, in his "History of Ireland," speaks of the royal seat of Tlachtga, where the Fire Tlachtga was ordained to be kindled. He says:—The use of this sacred fire was to summon the Priests, the Augurs, and Druids of Ireland to repair thither and assemble upon the Eve of All Saints, in order to consume the sacrifices that were offered to their Pagan Gods; and it was established under the penalty of a great fine, that no other fire should be kindled upon that night throughout the kingdom; so that the fire that was to be used in the country, was to be derived from this holy fire; for which privilege the people were to pay a *Scraball*, which amounts to threepence every year as an acknowledgment to the King of Munster, because the palace of Tlachtga, where this fire burned, was the proportion taken from the province of Munster, and added to the country of Meath.

The second royal palace that was erected was in the proportion taken from the province of Conacht, and here was a general convocation assembled of all the inhabitants of the kingdom that were able to appear, which was called the Convocation of Visneach, and kept upon the first day of May, where they offered sacrifices to the principal deity in the island, whom they adored under the name of Beul. Upon this occasion they were used to kindle two fires in every territory in the kingdom, in honour of this pagan god. It was a solemn ceremony at this time to drive a number of cattle of every kind between these fires;

this was conceived to be an antidote and a preservation
against the murrain, or any other pestilential distemper
among cattle for the year following; and from these fires
that were made in worship of the god Beul, the day upon
which the Christian festival of St. Philip and St. James is
observed, is called in the Irish language Beul-tinne. The
derivation of the word is thus: La in Irish signifies a day,
Beul is the name of the pagan deity, and Teinne is the
same with fire in the English, which words, when they are
pronounced together, sound La Beultinne."

Leslie in his "Early Races of Scotland," says: "From
Dondera Head in Ceylon to the Himalaya Mountains, and
from the borders of China to the extremities of Western
Europe and its islands, we find clear evidence of the
former prevalence of the earliest form of false worship, viz.,
the adoration of light, the sun, and 'the whole host of
heaven.' In the Rajpoot state of Marwar, in its capital
Udayayoor, 'The City of the Rising Sun!' the precedence
of Surya, the sun god, is still maintained. The sacred
standard of the country bears his image, and the Raja,
claiming to be his descendant, appears as his representative."

"In a complicated form the Parsees of British India
still retain that worship of light, symbolised in the sun
and fire, for which they became exiles when their faith was
proscribed in the land of their ancestors."

Leslie quotes various authors and travellers who had
personally witnessed the remains of many of these altars.
"Chardin," he says, "in his travels in Media in the end
of the seventeenth century describes circles of large stones
that must have been brought a distance of six leagues to
the place where he observed them. The tradition regarding
these circles was, that councils were there held, each member of the assembly being seated on a separate stone." *

In the Persian province of Fars, Sir William Ouseley
observed a monolith ten or twelve feet high, surrounded by
a fence of stones. This rude column had a cavity on the
top. Similiar instances—viz., of monoliths having a cavity
in the top—existed among the primitive monuments of
Scotland. (In Kincardineshire, at Auchincorthie, there were

* Chardin's Voyages, vol. ii.

five circles of stones. On the top of one of the stones which stood on the east side of the largest circle, there was a hollow three inches deep, along the bottom of which, and down the side of the stone, a channel was cut. Another of the stones in this group had a similar cavity and channel. Other examples of such artificial cavities in ancient British monuments could be pointed out.—(Gibson's Camden, vol. ii., p. 291.) The same traveller remarked a few old trees which grew near this column, and these he supposed to be the remains of a consecrated grove. One of the trees was thickly hung with rags, the native offerings of the inhabitants of the country. Trees with such garniture may commonly be observed in the Dekhan and other parts of India, and not long since might be seen in many places in Britain. The Monolith thus described, and adjacent to the grove, was called by an expression equivalent to "Stone of the Fire Temple." We know from Herodotus that the ancient Persians, like their expatriated descendants the Parsees, were worshippers of the sun and fire, and the mysterious rites of the heathen inhabitants of Britain must have closely resembled those of the Persians, when the similarity induced Pliny to remark that Britain cultivates magic with ceremonial so august that it might be supposed that the art was first communicated from them to the people of Persia.

Turning to Herodotus as here suggested, speaking of the order given by Cambyses to burn the corpse of Amasis, after his people had failed to tear it apart, owing to its having been embalmed, the historian says:—"This was truly an impious command to give, for the Persians hold fire to be a god, and never by any chance burn their dead. Indeed this practice is unlawful, both with them and with the Egyptians—with them for the reason above mentioned, since they deem it wrong to give the corpse if a man to a god; and with the Egyptians, because they believe fire to be a live animal, which eats whatever it can seize, and then glutted with the food, dies with the matter it feeds upon." *

Leslie says "it is important, as a prelude to the description of rites in a worship common to the early inhabitants of the Indian Peninsula and to the Celtic population of Gaul

* Thalia, 16, Rawlinson.

and Britain, to refer to the cognate expressions which they employed for the object of their adoration. In Cingalese, Ja, Jwala, signifies light, lustre, flame; Jwalana, light; also Agni, or personified and deified fire. Eliya is also Cingalese for light; in Welsh, Lleuer and Lleuad, the moon; in Gaelic, Eibhle, anything on fire. In Sanscrit, Jwala signifies light, flame; in Cornish, Gwawl; in Welsh, Goleu; in Armorican, Goleu. In Gaelic, Geal and Eallaidhe is white; Soillse, light, sunlight; Suil, the eye. In Cingalese, Haili and Hel, and in Sanscrit, Heli or Helis is the sun. In Welsh it is Haul, pronounced Hail; in Armorican, Haul and Heol; in Cornish, Houl and Heul. The great festival of heathen Britain—viz, Yeul—was celebrated at that period of the year when the sun having obtained the greatest distance from the earth, commenced his return to restore warmth and to revivify nature. Although Christmas superseded the heathen festival, not only the ancient name of Yeul, but many of the customs, evidently connected with the heathen rites, are not yet obsolete in South Britain; and in Scotland, at least in the more remote parts, and in agricultural districts, Yeul is still the word in general use for Christmas Day."

Hone, in his "Every-day Book" vol. I. p. 204, says: "The Yeul feast and Yeul log can be clearly traced to their original source. The blaze of lights, and the kindling of the great Yule log on Christmas Eve by a portion of the Yule brand of the former year, is as clearly a heathen ceremony, and for the same object of worship, as the fires on Midsummer Eve. As to the feast, in times comparatively recent, the Greenlanders held a sun-feast at the winter solstice, to rejoice in the commencement of returning light and warmth."

"From Teinidh and Tein, Irish and Gaelic for fire, is probably derived the obsolete English word 'to teend.' Herrich, speaking of the Christmas brand, says part must be kept wherewith to *teend* the Christmas by next year."

Evidence of some sort of fire-worship in England at various times is to be found in the *Confessional* of Ecgbert, Archbishop of York (8th century) and the Penitential of Theodore, Archbishop of Canterbury (7th century), and that this included the adoration of the light of the sun and moon seems probable from the prohibition of the practice of passing children through fire extending to that of exposing them on the house-tops for the benefit of their health.

Leslie remarks that it is curious to compare these restrictions and penalties to be enforced by English ecclesiastical authorites with the denunciation of the same heathen practices by the prophet Zephaniah, (Chap. I., 4, 5.) "I will cut off the remnant of Baal, and them that worship the host of heaven upon the house-tops."

The allusion to the Midsummer Eve Fire in Ilone, reminds us of the "Fire of Bel" or Beltane of Scotland, a festival generally celebrated on May-day old style. Leslie says, in other Celtic countries of Western Europe the same expression, with slight variations in sound, was also used for the great heathen festival which was held about the beginning of the month of May. He further says:—"Beltane is also used to express the fires that were kindled in honour of Bel on that and on other days connected with his worship, as on Midsummer Eve, afterwards called the vigil of St. John, on All-Hallowe'en, and on Yeule, which is now Christmas. Of the ceremonies practised at Beltane, and continued almost to our own times, the most remarkable and general were the fires lighted in honour of Bel."

"Kindling fires at Beltane, on the hills and conspicuous places in level districts, was so universal in Scotland—also in Ireland and Cornwall—that it is unnecessary to refer to records for proof of events which may still be witnessed in this year 1865.

"Conjoined with Apollo in the inscription on a Roman altar found at Inveresk is an epithet bearing a considerable resemblance to the name of the sun in Gaelic. Apollini-Granno is the commencement of the inscription. Grian or Greine is the sun in Gaelic, and Grianach is 'the sunny.' This resemblance it is as well to notice, for epithets not similar in sound but identical in meaning are used for Apollo or the sun by classic authors and the Scottish Celts, as Gruagach, the fair-haired. Enclosures called Grianan or Greinham, 'the house of the sun,' where the people worshipped the sun, are to be met with everywhere. On the Gruagach stones libations of milk were poured. A clergyman of the Western Isles says that about a century ago (this was in 1774), Gruagach got credit for being the father of a child at Shulista, near Duntulme, the seat of M'Donald. Gruagach, the sun, was represented by certain rude stones of large size. On the island of Bernera, in the parish of

F

Harris, a circle, defined by long sharp pointed stones, has in the centre a stone in the form of an inverted pyramid, called Clach-na-Greine, 'the stone of the sun.'"

Toland, in his "History of Druids," gathers together a good deal of important information relative to Fire Customs in various parts of England, Ireland, Scotland, and Wales, and the adjacent islands. He speaks of the carns (cairns) or heaps of stones which are found on mountain tops and other eminencies in different localities, and after alluding to the uses they served in course of time as beacons, being conveniently situated for such a purpose, says—"They were originally designed for fires of another nature. The fact stood thus. On May-eve the Druids made prodigious fires on those carns, which being every one in sight, could not but afford a glorious show over a whole nation. These fires were in honour of Beal or Bealan, latinised by the Roman authors into Belenus, by which name the Gauls and their colonies understood the sun: and, therefore, to this hour the first day of May is by the aboriginal Irish called La Bealteine, or the day of Belen's fire."

"May-day is likewise called La Bealteine by the High-landers of Scotland, who are no contemptible part of the Celtic offspring. So it is in the Isle of Man ; and in Armoric a priest is still called Belec, or the Servant of Bel, and priesthood Belegieth. Two such fires as we have mentioned were kindled by one another on May-eve in every village of the nation (as well throughout all Gaul, as in Britain, Ireland, and the adjoining lesser islands), between which fires the men and the beasts to be sacrificed were to pass ; from whence came the proverb, *Between Bel's two fires,* meaning one in a great strait, not knowing how to extricate himself. One of the fires was on the carn, another on the ground. On the eve of the first day of November there were also such fires kindled, accompanied (as they constantly were) with sacrifices and feasting. These November fires were in Ireland called Tine tlach'd gha, from tlach'd-gha, a place hence so called in Meath where the Archdruid of the realm had his fire on the said eve ; and for which piece of ground, because originally belonging to Munster, but appointed by the supreme monarch for this use, there was an annual acknowledgement (called sgreaboll) paid to the king of that province.

"On the aforesaid eve all the people of the country,
out of a religious persuasion instilled into them by the Druids,
extinguished their fires as entirely as the Jews are wont to
sweep their houses the night before the feast of unleavened
bread. Then every master of a family was religiously obliged
to take a portion of the consecrated fire home, and to kindle
the fire anew in his house, which for the ensuing year was
to be lucky and prosperous. He was to pay, however, for
his future happiness whether the event proved answerable or
not; and though his house should be afterwards burnt, yet
he must deem it the punishment of some new sin, or ascribe
it to anything rather than to want of virtue in the consecration of the fire, or of validity in the benediction of the
Druid, who, from officiating at the carns, was likewise called
Cairnech, a name that continued to signify priest even in
Christian times. But if any man had not cleared with the
Druids for the last year's dues, he was neither to have a
spark of this holy fire from the carns, nor durst any of his
neighbours let him take the benefit of theirs under pain of
excommunication, which, as managed by the Druids, was
worse than death. If he would brew, therefore, or bake, or
roast, or boil, or warm himself and family; in a word, if
he would live the winter out, the Druid's dues must be paid
by the last of October, so that this trick alone was more
effectual than are all the Acts of Parliament made for
securing our present clergy's dues.

"As to the fire-worship which (by the way) prevailed
over all the world, the Celtic nations kindled other fires on
Midsummer-eve, which are still continued by the Roman
Catholics of Ireland; making them in all their grounds, and
carrying flaming brands about their corn-fields. This they
do likewise all over France and in some of the Scottish
Isles. These midsummer fires and sacrifices were to obtain
a blessing on the fruits of the earth, now becoming ready
for gathering; as those of the first of May, that they might
prosperously grow; and those of the last of October were a
thanksgiving for finishing their harvest. But in all of them
regard was also had to the several degrees of increase and
decrease in the heat of the sun's rays."

With regard to the proverb "Between Bel's two fires,"
Mr. Huddleston in his new edition of Toland (1814) adds
a note in which he says:—"As Mr. Toland in his note on

this passage, informs us the Irish phrase is Ittir dha theine
Bheil; Dr. Smith has also given us the Scottish phrase,
Gabha Bheil, *i.e.*, the jeopardy of Bel. Both agree that
these expressions denote one in the most imminent danger.
Mr. Toland says the men and beasts to be sacrificed passed
between two fires, and that hence the proverb originated.
Dr. Smith, on the contrary, imagines that this was one of
the Druidical ordeals whereby criminals were tried; and
instead of making them pass betwixt the fires, makes them
march directly across them. Indeed, he supposed the Druids
were kind enough to anoint the feet of the criminals, and
render them invulnerable to the flames. If so there could
have been neither danger nor trial. It may also be remarked,
that had the doctor's hypothesis been well founded, there
was no occasion for two fires, whereas by the phrase, *between
Bel's two fires*, we know that two were used. Doctor Smith
has evidently confounded the Gabha Bheil with a feat
practised by the Hirpins on Mount Soracte."

It seems that the expression used by the Scotch expressive of a man in difficulties, "He is between the two
fires of Bel," was common enough to attract the attention of
other writers than those we have cited, and of most travellers
in the Highlands. Martin mentions it in his "Western
Isles," as also Shaw and the Rev. D. M'Queen. The latter
is cited by Leslie as a Gaelic scholar of the last century,
who in regard to the expression, "He is betwixt two Beltein
fires," gives as an explanation that the Celtic tribes in their
sacred enclosures offered sacrifices, commonly horses, that were
burnt between two large fires, and Leslie adds, "On this
it may be remarked that horses were sacrificed to the sun
by the Arian race from the earliest times; and this continued to be practised by Hindus, Persians, and other nations.
In Britain it is probable that our heathen ancestors sacrificed
horses, and it is certain that they ate them."

Jamieson's splendid "Etymological Dictionary of the
Scottish Language," supplies us with valuable information on
the point we are discussing, drawn from a variety of reliable
authorities. Under "BELTANE, Beltein, the name of a sort
of festival observed on the first day of May, O.S.;" we
have:—"A town in Perthshire, on the borders of the Highlands, is called *Tillie-* (or *Tullie*) *beltane, i.e.* the eminence
or rising ground of the fire of Baal. In the neighbourhood

is a druidical temple of eight upright stones, where it is supposed the fire was kindled. At some distance from this is another temple of the same kind, but smaller, and near it a well still held in great veneration. On Beltane morning superstitious people go to this well, and drink of it; then they make a procession round it, as I am informed, nine times. After this, they in like manner go round the temple. So deep rooted is this heathenish superstition in the minds of many who reckon themselves good Protestants, that they will not neglect these rites, even when Beltane falls on Sabbath."

Quoting from P. Loudon, Statist. Acc. iii., 105, the writer proceeds:—"The custom still remains [in the West of Scotland] among the herds and young people to kindle fires in the high grounds, in honour of Beltan. *Beltan*, which in Gaelic signifies *Baal* or *Bel's fire*, was anciently the time of this solemnity. It is now kept on St. Peter's Day."

Just here we may turn to Mr. Pennant's "Tour in Scotland," for the following interesting particulars. "On the first of May, the herdsmen of every village hold their Beltein, a rural sacrifice. They cut a square trench on the ground, leaving the turf in the middle; on that they make a fire of wood, on which they dress a large caudle of eggs, butter, oatmeal, and milk; and bring, besides the ingredients of the caudle, plenty of beer and whisky; for each of the company must contribute something. The rites begin with spilling some of the caudle on the ground by way of libation: on that every one takes a cake of oatmeal, upon which are raised nine square knobs, each dedicated to some particular being, the supposed preserver of their flocks and herds, or to some particular animal, the real destroyer of them: each person then turns his face to the fire, breaks off a knob, and flinging it over his shoulder, says—*This I give to thee, preserve thou my horses; this to thee, preserve thou my sheep;* and so on. After that they use the same ceremony to the noxious animals; *This I give to thee, O Fox! spare thou my lambs; this to thee, O hooded Crow! this to thee, O Eagle!*" *

Further on the same traveller writes:—"The Beltein, or

* Pennant, vol. I., p. 111.

the rural sacrifice on the first of May, O.S., has been mentioned before. Hallow-eve is also kept sacred : as soon as it is dark, a person sets fire to a bush of broom fastened round a pole, and attended with a crowd, runs round the village. He then flings it down, keeps a great quantity of combustible matters in it, and makes a great bonfire. A whole tract is thus illuminated at the same time, and makes a fine appearance. The carrying of the fiery pole appears to be a relic of Druidism." *

The " Statistical Account of Scotland, Parish of Callander, Perths," supplies several important and interesting facts re-lating to this. " The people of this district have two customs which are fast wearing out, not only here, but all over the Highlands, and therefore ought to be taken notice of while they remain. Upon the first day of May, which is called *Beltau* or *Baltein Day*, all the boys in a township or hamlet meet in the moors. They cut a table in the green sod, of a round figure, by casting a trench in the ground of such cir-cumference as to hold the whole company. They kindle a fire, and dress a repast of eggs and milk in the consistence of a custard. They knead a cake of oatmeal, which is toasted at the embers against a stone. After the custard is eaten up, they divide the cake into so many portions, as similar as possible to one another in size and shape, as there are persons in the company. They daub one of these portions all over with charcoal, until it be perfectly black. They put all the bits of cake into a bonnet. Every one, blind-fold, draws out a portion. He who holds the bonnet is entitled to the last bit. Whoever draws the black bit is the devoted person who is to be sacrificed to Baal, whose favour they mean to implore, in rendering the year productive of the sustenance of man and beast. There is little doubt of these inhuman sacrifices having been once offered in this country, as well as in the east, although they now pass from the act of sacrificing, and only compel the devoted person to leap three times through the flames ; with which the ceremonies of this festival are closed."

Again referring to Jamieson, he says :—" The respect paid by the ancient Britons to Belus, or Belinus, is evident from the names of some of their kings. As the Babylonians had their *Beletis* or *Belibus*, *Rige-Belus*, *Merodoch-Baladan* and *Belshazzar*; the Tyrians their *Ich-baals* and *Balator*, the Britons had their *Cassi-belin*, and their *Cuno-belin.*

The Gael and Ir. word *Beal-tine* or *Beil-teine* signifies *Belus' Fire*; as composed of Baal or Belis, one of the names of the sun in Gaul, and *tein* signifying fire. Even in Angus a spark of fire is called a *tein* or *teind.*"

Martin's Western Islands bears similar testimony, thus :— "Another god of the Britons was Belus or Belinus, which seems to have been the Assyrian god Bel, or Belus ; and probably from this Pagan deity comes the Scots' term of Beltin—having its first rise from the custom practised by the Druids in the isles, of extinguishing all the fires in the parish until the tythes were paid ; and upon payment of them, the fires were kindled in each family, and never till then. In those days malefactors were burnt between two fires ; hence when they would express a man in a great strait, they say, He is between two fires of Bel, which in their language they express thus, Edir da hin Veaul or Bel."

It has been remarked that the Pagan rites of the festival of Midsummer Eve, the Summer Solstice may be considered as a counterpart of those used at the Winter Solstice of Yule-tide. "There is one thing," says Brand, "that seems to prove this beyond the possibility of a doubt. In the old Runic Fasti, a wheel was used to denote the festival of Christmas. Thus Durandus, when speaking of the Rites of the Feast of St. John Baptist, informs us of this curious circumstance, that in some places they roll a wheel about to signify that the Sun, then occupying the highest place in the Zodiac, is beginning to descend ; and in the amplified account given by Naogeorgus, we read that this wheel was taken up to the top of a mountain and rolled down from thence ; and that, as it had been previously covered with straw, twisted about it and set on fire, it appeared at a distance as if the sun had been falling from the sky. And he further observes, that the people imagine that all their ill-luck rolls away from them together with this wheel."

"Leaping over the fires is mentioned among the super-stitious rites used at the Palilia in Ovid's Fasti. The Palilia were feasts instituted in honour of Pales, the goddess of shepherds (though Varro makes Pales masculine), on the

calends of May. In order to drive away wolves from the
folds, and distempers from the cattle, the shepherds on this
day kindled several heaps of straw in their fields, which they
leaped over."

"Bourne tells us that it was the custom in his time,
in the North of England, chiefly in country villages, for old
and young people to meet together and be merry over a
large fire, which was made for that purpose in the open
street. This, of whatever materials it consisted, was called
a Bone-fire. Over and about this fire they frequently leap,
and play at various games such as running, wrestling,
dancing, &c.; this, however, is generally confined to the
younger sort; for the old ones, for the most part, sit by
as spectators only, and enjoy themselves over their bottle,
which they do not quit till midnight, and sometimes till
cock-crow the next morning."

A correspondent of the *Gentleman's Magazine* for February, 1795, writing from Skye, gives us:—"Curious fact
relating to the worship of Baal in Ireland. The Irish have
ever been worshippers of fire, and of Baal, and are so to
this day. The chief festival in honour of the sun and fire,
is upon the twenty-first of June, when the sun arrives at
the Summer Solstice, or rather begins its retrograde move-
ment. I was so fortunate, in the summer of 1782, as to
have my curiosity gratified by a sight of this ceremony over
a very great extent of country. At the house where I was
entertained, it was told me that we should see at midnight
the most singular sight in Ireland, which was the lighting
of Fires in honour of the Sun. Accordingly, exactly at
midnight, the Fires began to appear; and taking the ad-
vantage of going up to the leads of the house, which had
a widely-extended view, I saw on a radius of thirty miles,
all around, the Fires burning on every eminence which the
country afforded. I had a farther satisfaction, in learning
from undoubted authority, that the people danced round the
Fires, and at the close went through these Fires, and made
their sons and daughters, together with their cattle, pass
through the Fire; and the whole was conducted with
religious solemnity. This account is exceedingly curious, and
though I forbear the mention of names, I can venture to
assure you that it is authentic."

The remarks of Borlase in his "Antiquities of Cornwall," come in here very suitably. He says—"Of the fires we kindle in many parts of England, at some stated time of the year, we know not certainly the rise, reason or occasion, but they may probably be reckoned among the relicks of the Druid superstitious fires. In Cornwall, the festival fires called Bonfires, are kindled on the Eve of St. John the Baptist and St. Peter's Day; and Midsummer is thence, in the Cornish tongue, called 'Golnan,' which signifies both light and rejoicing. At these fires the Cornish attend with lighted torches, tarred and pitched at the end, and make their perambulations round their fires, and go from village to village carrying their torches before them, and this is certainly the remains of the Druid superstition, for 'faces præferre,' to carry lighted torches, was reckoned a kind of Gentilism, and as such particularly prohibited by the Gallick Councils. They were in the eye of the law 'accensores facularum,' and thought to sacrifice to the devil, and to deserve capital punishment."

Brand mentions a few additional particulars which we here transcribe.

"Torreblanca, in his 'Demonology,' has a passage in which he tells us how the ancients were accustomed to pass their children of both sexes through the fire for the sake of securing them a prosperous and fortunate lot, and he adds that the Germans imitated this profane usage in their Midsummer pyres in honour of the anniversary of St. John's Day.

"Moresin appears to have been of opinion that the custom of leaping over these fires is a vestige of the ordeal, where to be able to pass through fires with safety was held to be an indication of innocence. To strengthen the probability of this conjecture, we may observe that not only the young and vigorous, but even those of grave characters used to leap over them, and there was an interdiction of ecclesiastical authority to deter clergymen from this superstitious instance of agility. A note at the foot of the page says that Mr. Brand saw in the possession of Douce, a French print, entitled 'L'este le Feu de la St. Jean,' from the hand of Mariette. In the centre was the fire made of wood piled up very regularly, and having a tree stuck up in the midst of it. Young men and women were represented dancing round it hand in hand. Herbs were stuck in their hats and caps, and garlands of the same surrounded their waists or were slung across their shoulders.

"In the 'Traite des Superstitions,' we read 'Whoever desires to know the colour of his future wife's hair, has only to walk three times round the fire of St. John, and when the fire is half extinguished he must take a brand, let it go out, and then put it under his pillow, and the next morning he will find encircling it threads of hair of the desired colour.' But this must be done with the eyes shut. We are further told, where there is a widow or a marriageable girl in a house, it is necessary to be very careful not to remove the brands, as this drives away lovers.

"The third Council of Constantinople, A.D. 680, in its sixty-fifth canon, enacted the following interdiction :—'Those Bonefires that are kindled by certaine people on New Moones before their shops and houses, over which also they do foolishly leape, by a certaine ancient custome, we command them from henceforth to cease. Whoever, therefore, shall doe any such thing; if he be a clergyman, let him be deposed ; if a layman, let him be excommunicated. For, in the Fourth Book of the Kings it is written : And Manasseh built an altar to all the host of heaven, in the two courts of the Lord's house, and made his children to passe through the Fire, &c.' Prynne observes upon this : 'Bonefires, there-fore, had their originall from this idolatrous custome, as this Generall Councell hath defined; therefore all Christians should avoid them.' And the Synodus Francica under Pope Zachary, A.D. 742, inhibits 'those sacrilegious Fires which they call *Nedfri* (or Bonefires), and all other observations of the Pagans whatsoever.'"

CHAPTER VII.

Paradise Lost and Moloch—The God of the Ammonites—The slaughter of Children by Fire, notices in the Scriptures— Fire Ceremonies and Moloch—Sacred Fires of the Phœnicians — The Carthaginians — Custom of the Oziese — Sardinian Customs and Moloch—The Cuthites—Persian Fire Worship— The House-Fires of Greece and Rome—Sacred Books of the East—Laws of Manu—The Rig Veda and Hymns to Agni, the God of Fire—Vesta, worship of—The Magi—Zoroaster.

IN Milton's "Paradise Lost" we read :—

"First, Moloch, horrid king, besmeared with blood
Of human sacrifice, and parents' tears;
Though for the noise of drums and timbrels loud,
Their children's cries unheard, that passed through fire,
To his grim idol. Him the Ammonite
Worshipped in Rabba and her watery plain,
In Argob and in Basan, to the stream
Of utmost Arnon : nor content with such
Audacious neighbourhood, the wisest heart
Of Solomon he led by fraud to build
His temple right against the temple of God,
On that opprobrious hill, and made his grove
The pleasant valley of Hinnom, Tophet thence
And black Gehenna called, the type of Hell."

"Moloch was the god of the Ammonites. In the worship and sacrifices in his honour they burnt their sons and daughters, with the accustomed forms and ceremonies." In Leviticus xviii. 21 we find a prohibition of passing the children through the fire and in chapter xx. the punishment of death by stoning is awarded to any who gave their seed to Moloch.

"However," says Selden, "many of the Hebrews write that the children were neither burnt nor slain, but that two funeral pyres were constructed by the priests of Moloch, and that they led the children only between the pyres, as if in this way to purify them. Moses Ben Maimon says that in those days the servitors of the fires made men believe that their sons and daughters would die unless they were thus

led, and on this account and the love of their children they
hastened to do that which was so easy, and there was no
other way of saving the children from the fire. There are
some who say that the father in due form delivered the
child to the priests to be given back, and that he led it
through, carrying it on his shoulders. It is nevertheless
true that the children were not only led between the fires,
but were also burnt in the sacrifices of the idols. See
Psalm cvi. 37 and 38, and read, "Yea, they sacrificed their
sons and their daughters unto devils, and shed innocent
blood, even the blood of their sons and their daughters,
whom they sacrificed unto the idols of Canaan, and the land
was polluted with the blood."

Philastrius says "that they placed an altar in the valley
of the children of Hinnom, and so called after the name of
a certain Tophet, and in that place the Jews sacrificed their
sons and daughters to demons." There are other places
which sufficiently indicate immolation of children in those
regions of Syria where Moloch was adored. Thus, see Wisdom
of Solomon, xii. 5, "And also those merciless murders of
children and devourers of men's flesh, the feasts of blood;"
and xiv. 23, "For whilst they slew their children in
sacrifices"; and Jeremiah vii. 31, says "And they have built
the high places of Tophet, which is in the valley of the
son of Hinnom, to burn their sons and their daughters in
the fire." See also nineteenth chapter, verse 5; Ezekiel xvi.
20, 21, and xxiii, 37 and 39. From this affair perhaps
arose the delusion of the Greeks and Hebrews that, by
another ancient rite, they who took an oath were accustomed
to pass through fire, as if by escaping from injury their
words would be proved true. The learned Paul Fagius, in
speaking of him, says, "The statue of Moloch was such that
it had seven hollow chambers. One was open for meal
offerings, another for turtle doves, the third for sheep, the
fourth for the ram, the fifth for the calf, the sixth for the
bull, and a seventh was open for him who wished to offer
his child." The face of the idol was the same as that of
the calf, and the hands were evidently disposed and arranged
conveniently to receive from the bystanders all that was
offered. While the child was burning in the blazing fire,
they danced about and beat drums to drown the horrible
cries and lamentations, There is a question whether the

author of these seven hollow chambers did not learn it
from the sacred rites of the Persian Mithra, for he also had
seven sacred doors, which referred to the number of the
planets, and men, women and children were likewise sacrificed
to him.

It was necessary to such as were initiated to this god
to pass through eighty kinds of sufferings, that is, through
fire and cold and most serious dangers of every kind, before
they could be received as epoptas, or regularly initiated.
It is proper to add that neither elsewhere than in Moloch
will be found Adrammelech and Anammelech, the gods of
Sepharvaim.   See II. Kings xviii. 31 : "And they burnt
their children in fire to Adrammelech and Anammelech, the
gods of Sepharvaim." His priests, who were also frequently
the priests of other gods, were called Cemerin.   This word
in the Chaldee dialect Comeraja, is everywhere in the Targum
substituted for priests of idolatry.   In II. Kings xxiii. 10,
it reads, "And he (Josiah) defiled Topheth, which is in the
valley of the children of Hinnom, that no man might make
his son or his daughter pass through the fire to Moloch."
The valley of the children of Hinnom, which in Hebrew is
gi ber Hinnom, was a field near the city, and is so called
from the groans or lamentations of the children while they
were burning.   Hinnom is from the Hebrew word nahmen,
and means that he groans or gnashed his teeth from intense
pain.   That place is watered by the streams of Siloe, and in
the time of St. Jerome was beautiful, and ornamented with
shady groves and delightful gardens.   And there he remarks
"that it was a custom among other nations to select the
head of streams and groves for sacred rites."   But the word
Tophet is from the Hebrew Toph, that is, "they ask for a
drum," which was beaten and loudly sounded in the vicinity
to prevent the parents hearing the most doleful lamentations
and wailings of their children while the sacred rites were
performing.

Moloch is also called Baal.   See Jeremiah xix. 5., "They
have built also the high places of Baal to burn their sons
with fire."   He is also called Milcolm in Kings xi. 5., "For
Solomon went after Ashtoreth the goddess of the Zidonians,
and after Milcolm the abominations of the Ammonites."   And
Luke, in Acts viii. 43., says, "Yea, ye took up the tabernacle
of Molech."   The Syrians and Arabians call it Melcom.   In

many oriental languages Melech, means king, Milcom means their king, and Malcecem, our king, and both words in sacred scripture designate Moloch. To him reference is had in Zephaniah i. 5., "And them that worship and swear by the Lord, and that swear by Melcham," because Moloch was especially worshipped under the name of king. As thus Baal means Lord, and as Melech or Molech or Moloch means king, they denote this god of the Ammonites; and it is perhaps, he himself who, in the most ancient theology of the Phœnicians, was often called by the singular title of king of gods. He was also called Adodus, and was worshipped by the Syrians not only as Adad-Hadad and Benhadad (and which could readily pass into Adodus), but the very name Adad was propagated continually for ten generations in their royal families. These names, and Bedad, Hedar Mesahab, and Ahab, will be found in Genesis xxxvi. and I Kings xx. Macrobius, speaking of the Syrians and this god Adodus and king of gods, says, "They gave to the god whom they venerate as the highest and the greatest the name Adad, and which means unus or one. Hada or Chada is a god of the female sex, and agrees with Adardaga or Atergatis, and was worshipped in that name in the neighourhood of Syria. Heseychius says that Hada was the goddess of Juno, and Adad a god and the sun. But Hadad very well denotes the clamour or loud noise of persons exhorting; neither is it altogether unlike the lamentations of children in the sacrifices to Moloch. And ancient writers say that the effigies of both Adad and Moloch were the same, and fashioned for expressing the sun.

Theophylactus says "that the bright shining stone in the image of Phosphorus he understands to be the sun." All these are very proper for the sun, the king of gods or stars, and which he also thought who made the first mention of the seven hollow chambers in the statue of Moloch. In the same number is ascribed to Mithra, who by the unanimous consent of antiquity, and especially of the ancient inscriptions, is regarded as being the same as the sun, shines with many colours. But Mithri, Mithir or Mether, in Persian, signifies dynasty or lord, and this is also one of the titles of Moloch.

Saturn among the Latins, and Chronos among the Greeks, is oft-times considered to be Moch. Infants or children were victims common to both, and that nefarious sacred rite would seem to have migrated from Syria into Europe and Africa. Pescennius Festus says "that the Carthaginians were accustomed to offer human victims to Saturn, and when they were overcome in battle by Agathocles, king of the Siculi, he (the king) believed that his god was angry with him, and, therefore, that he might diligently make the necessary expiation, he immolated to this god two hundred children of the nobility. Those who had no children were forced to buy them from the poor."

Tertullian writes:—"That impious custom continued in Africa down to the times of Tiberias." These sacred rites of the Phœnicians proceeded from those of the Syrians, as the solemn use of fifes and drums among them will prove. For the lamentations of the children or parents among those about to be sacrificed is held to be an atonement. It is almost certain that by the name of Moloch this God was worshipped in like manner among the Carthaginians.

The Carthaginians worshipped Amilear, and that name comes from the same source as Molech. Both words are pure Hebrew or Punic, if you regard their etymology, and they mean king, or perhaps Ameliar may be queen, that is, may mean Basilia, queen of the Atlantians, and which may refer to Celestis, queen of the Carthaginians. For as among them Bel or Uranus is a god, and Cœlestis a goddess, so Uranus and Basilia may be a god and goddess among them. And from the same source we must look for the name of Milicus, the father-in-law of Hannibal, and of his daughter Imilcis, which is queen, and of Imilco, a Carthaginian general. Melech means king, and Malcha queen, which they pronounce Molicus and Imilcis. Strabo says "that Hercules, worshipped among the Tyrians, was called Melcartos or Melcarthos. But he was the son of Jove Demaruns, and he is the same as the Phœnician and Carthaginian Hercules, who was appeased by human victims as Moloch was. The first part of his name was evidently derived from Melech of the Hebrews, for almost by the same word Hercules was known among the Amathusians. Amathus was a city of Phœnicia, and an island of the Phœnician sea adjoins Cyprus, and in it there is also a city called Amathus. The latter had sacred rites in common with the former. What the words Artos or Arthos in the name mean is not clear. Traces of it, however, are seen in the Punic names Bomilcar and

Hamilcar. In Bœotia, which retains many names which Cadmus brought with him from Phœnicia, there is a river and a city called Haliartus, named after the builder and discoverer. In Scolus there is likewise an image of Mega-lartus held in great esteem. Some think it is the image of the Megalartian Ceres, and derive it from the Greek word artos, which means bread, because she was the goddess of corn."

"But whatever the god was, his Phœnician origin is evident, for Cadmus, Ismenus, and Thebes were all Phœnician names, and perhaps the Hebrew word Aritz in artes passed into Melicartes, which some read Melicatus. Aritz means very strong, and thus Melicaritz signifies a strong king or tyrant, and the word could readily pass into Melicartos. Thence perhaps in the Persian language Artaioi is heroes, or those who in the olden periods made themselves par-ticularly illustrious, and the word with this idea is present in the names Artoxerxis and Artabasis. Hence in Persian, Artas meant great or illustrious, and Artana kingdoms, and Herodotus says that Artoxerxis means a great warrior.

"Among the ancient Persians and Syrians in customs and languages many things were common to both. The Persians are accounted among our Syrians now and then by European writers, and Babylon is called a Persian city.

"As to the horrid sacrifice, the slaying of children, its origin does not lie concealed if there is any truth in Phœnician annals. There is a tradition among them that Saturn, one of the most ancient kings of Phœnicia, and whom they called Israel in order that he might deliver his kingdom from the greatest peril of an impending war, to render the gods propitious, immolated an only begotten son of himself and wife Anobreta. He was first ornamented with the royal fillets, and then led to the altar built for that purpose, and a wicked posterity, not understanding the case or the circumstances, continued to follow his example."*

Among the many usages derived by the Sardes from their Phœnician ancestors, one of a singular character is still practised by the Oziese, of which Father Bresciani gives the following account :—"Towards the end of March, or the beginning of April, it is the custom for young men and

* Selden's Syrian Deities. Hauser's Translation.

women to agree together to fill the relation of godfathers
and godmothers of St. John, *compare e comare*—such is the
phrase—for the ensuing year. At the end of May the pro-
posed *comare*, having procured a segment of the bark of a
cork tree, fashions it in the shape of a vase, and fills it
with rich light mould in which are planted some grains of
barley or wheat. The vase being placed in the sunshine,
well watered and carefully tended, the seed soon germinates,
blades spring up, and, making a rapid growth, in the course
of twenty-one days—that is, before the eve of St. John—
the vase is filled by a spreading and vigorous plant of
young corn. It then receives the name of Hermes, or, more
commonly, of *Su Nennere*, from a Sarde word, which possibly
has the same signification as the Phœnician name of garden;
similar vases being called, in ancient times, the gardens of
Adonis."

Forester in his "Rambles in Corsica and Sardinia,"
quoting the above and remarking upon it says:—"On the
eve of St. John, the cereal vase, ornamented with ribbons,
is exposed on a balcony, decorated with garlands and flags.
Formerly, also a little image in female attire, or *phallic*
emblems moulded in clay, such as were exhibited in the
feasts of Hermes, were placed among the blades of corn;
but these representations have been so severely denounced
by the Church, that they are fallen into disuse. The young
men flock in crowds to witness the spectacle and attend the
maidens who come out to grace the feast. A great fire is
lit on the piazza, round which they leap and gambol, the
couple who have agreed to be St. John's *compare* completing
the ceremony in this manner:—The man is placed on one
side of the fire, the woman on the other, each holding
opposite ends of a stick extended over the burning embers,
which they pass rapidly backwards and forwards. This is
repeated three times, so that the hand of each party passes
thrice through the flames. The union being thus sealed,
the *comparatico* or spiritual alliance is considered perfect.
After that, the music strikes up, and the festival is concluded by dances, prolonged to a late hour of the night."

"Father Bresciani, La Marmora, and other writers,
justly consider the Nennere as one of the many relics of
the Phœnician colonisation of Sardinia. Every one knows
that the sun and moon, under various names such as Isis

and Osiris, Adonis and Astarte, were the principal objects of
worship in the east from the earliest times; the sun being
considered as the vivifying power of universal nature,
the moon represented as a female, deriving her light from
the sun, as the passive principle of production. The abstruse
doctrines on the origin of things, thus shadowed out by the
ancient seers, generated the grossest ideas, expressed in the
phallic emblems, the lewdness and obscenities mixed up in
the popular worship of the deified principles of all existence.
Of the prevalence in Sardinia of the Egypto-Phœnician
mythology, in times the most remote, no one who has
examined the large collection of relics in the Royal Museum
at Cagliari, or who consults the plates attached to La
Marmora's work, can entertain any doubt. But it is sur-
prising to find, among the usages of the Sardes at the
present day, a very exact representation of the rites of a
primitive religion, introduced into the island nearly thirty-
five years ago, though it now partakes more of the character
of a popular festival than a religious ceremony.

"One of the principal incidents in the *Sarde Nennere*
consists in the consecration of the spiritual relation between
the *compare* and *comare*, by their thrice crossing hands over
the fire in the ceremonies of St. John's Day. A still more
extraordinary vestige of the idolatrous rite of passing through
the fire, is said to be still subsisting among the customs of
the people of Logudoro, in the neighbourhood of Ozieri, and
in other parts of Sardinia.

"Of the worship of Moloch—*par excellence* the Syrian and
Phœnician god of fire—by the ancient Sardes, there is undoubted proof. We find among the prodigious quantity of
such relics, collected from all parts of the island, in the
Royal Museum at Cagliari, a statuette of this idol, supposed
to have been a household god. Its features are appalling:
great goggle eyes leer fiercely from their hollow sockets;
the broad nostrils seem ready to sniff the fumes of the
horrid sacrifice; a wide gaping mouth grins with rabid fury
at the supposed victim; dark plumes spring from the forehead, like horns, and expanded wings from each shoulder
and knee. The image brandishes a sword with the left hand,
holding in the right a small grate, formed of metal bars. It
would appear that, this being heated, the wretched victim
was placed on it, and then, scorched so that the fumes of

the disgusting incense savoured in the nostrils of the rabid idol, it fell upon a brazier of burning coals beneath, where it was consumed. There is another idol in this collection with the same truculent cast of features, but horned, and clasping a bunch of snakes in the right hand, a trident in the left, with serpents twined round its legs. This image has a large orifice in the belly, and flames are issuing between the ribs, so that it would appear that when the brazen image of the idol was thoroughly heated, the unhappy children intended for sacrifice were thrust into the mouth in the navel, and there grilled—savoury morsels, on which the idol seems, from its features, rabidly gloating, while the priests, we are told, endeavoured to drown the cries of the sufferers by shouts and the noise of drums and timbrels—

> '...... horrid king, besmeared with blood
> Of human sacrifice, and parents' tears;
> Though, for the noise of drums and timbrels loud,
> Their children's cries unheard, that passed through fire
> To his grim idol.'—*Par. Lost*, i. 392.

"This cruel child-sacrifice was probably the giving of his seed to Moloch, for which any Israelite or stranger that sojourned in Israel guilty of the crime was, according to the Mosaic law, to be stoned to death. We are informed in the Sacred Records that no such denunciations of the idolatries of the surrounding nations, no revelations of the attributes or teachings of the pure worship of Jehovah, restrained the Israelites from the practice of the foul and cruel rites of their heathen neighbours; and we find in the latter days of the Jewish Commonwealth the prophet Jeremiah predicting the desolation of the people for this sin among others, that they had estranged themselves from the worship of Jehovah, and burned incense to strange gods, and filled the holy place with the blood of innocents, and burned their sons and their daughters with fire for burnt-offerings unto Baal.

"There appear to have been two modes in which the ancient idolaters devoted their children to Moloch. In one they were sacrificed and consumed in the manner already descibed, a burnt offering to the idol for the expiation of the sins of their parents or their people. In the other they were only made to pass through the fire, in honour of the deity, and as a sort of initiation into his mysteries, and consecration to his service.

"Thus Ahaz, King of Judah, is said to have made his son to pass through the fire, according to the abominations of the heathen. And it is reckoned in the catalogue of the sins of Judah, which drew on them the vengeance of God, that they 'built the high places of Baal, to cause their sons and their daughters to pass through the fire unto Moloch.' *

"In the case of infants, it is supposed that this initiation, this 'baptism by fire' was performed either by placing them on a sort of grate suspended by chains from the vault of the temple, and passed rapidly over the sacred fire, or by the priests taking the infants in their arms and swaying them to and fro over or across the fire, chanting meanwhile certain prayers or incantations. With respect to children of older growth, they were made to leap naked through the fire before the idol, so that their whole bodies might be touched by the sacred flames, and purified, as it were, by contact with the divinity.

"The Sardes, we are informed by Father Bresciani, still preserve a custom representing this initiation by fire, but as in other Phœnician rites and practices, without the slightest idea of their profane origin. In the first days of spring, from one end of the island to the other, the villagers assemble and light great fires in the piazza and at the cross roads. The flames beginning to ascend, the children leap through them at a bound, so rapidly and with such dexterity that when the flames are highest it is seldom that their clothes or a hair of their head are singed. They continue this practice till the fuel is reduced to embers, the musicians meanwhile playing on the *lionedda* tunes adapted to a Phyrric dance. This, says the learned father, is a representation of the initiation through fire into the mysteries of Moloch." †

"Nergal, which is a Hebrew word, was, perhaps, a perpetual fire most religiously preserved in their Sefta, or sacred places. The Cuthites were so called from Cuthus, which was both the name of a river and region in Persia, and from which they were carried into Samaria in very large numbers. Strabo confirms the existence of the sacred fire in Persia in book fifteen. He says 'that in the temples

* Jeremiah xxxii. 35.

† See Bresciani and Forrester's Sardinia.

of the worshippers of Anaitis and Omanus, or Amanus, Persian gods among the Cappadocians, the care of the perpetual fire was committed to magi, who were called Pyrethri, or fire worshippers.' He further says, 'In that country there is a great multitude of them, and likewise many temples of the Persian gods; that they do not slay the victims with a knife, but with a certain kind of club, as pounding them to death with a pestle; that there were also certain chapels in which these fires were kept worthy of being remembered; that the altar was in the centre of the chapel, and upon which there were many cinders, and there the priests watched the inextinguishable fires; that they entered there daily, and sang or chanted for the space of almost an hour, at the same time holding a bundle of rods before the fire; that they were veiled in a woollen tiara, which, fitting well on all sides, covered their lips and jaws. These, which were built in their shrines, and which were called Pyratheia, were the eternal fires of the magi. That which they chanted was the theogony, or primeval history of the gods.'

"The Persians believed that every song was not equally efficacious in sacred rites. The rods seem to have been of tamarisk, and without a magus no kind of sacrifices were performed. In the other sacred rites it was an annual custom for the magi to hold the tamarisk while they chanted the theogony, as it was the habit of the ancient poets while singing to carry laurel in their hands. For this reason some believed that they were called rhapsodists, from the Greek word rhabdos, which means a rod. While chanting they stirred the fires with their rods and increased the flames. That which the ancients write is true regarding the institutions of the Persians, that any one who was about to become a king should be initiated into the magic rites, and that Ninus could not be more a king than a magus from that custom. The Persians received these sacred rites from the most ancient Chaldeans, and the latter called them Nergal, from two Hebrew words, nir and gal, which may mean either the fountain of fire or light, or fire or versatile light, and especially that inextinguishable fire which they watched in their holy places as the symbol of the sun. And although there were many gods in Persia, yet fire was worshipped by them before and above all other gods, and

in every sacrifice they especially invoked him as the Romans
did Janus. And hence, bound by religion, they did not
dare to pollute fire destined for daily uses with any un-
cleanliness. The Pyratheia, or fires, were called Pyreia by
others. Suidas says that Heraclius destroyed the Persian
cities and overthrew their Pyreia. But so ancient do the
Hebrews make the worship of fire among the Chaldeans,
that Ur of the Chaldeans, mentioned in Genesis xi., they
took for their fire god. Neither do the writings of the
ancients quoted by Maimonides prove anything else than
that fire was held in so much honour because it was a
symbol of the sun. In regard to this most ancient worship
in Chaldæa he thus discourses in 'More Nebochim,' book
three, chapter thirty:—'It is known that Abraham was
born among a people who served fire, and who, in their
credulity, believed there was no other god except the stars,
and I will in this chapter make you acquainted with their
books, which are not found with us translated in the
Arabic language. In their narrations and ancient contentions
you will know their reasons and opinions. Their credulity
is proved to you in their worship of the stars which they
believed to be gods, and that the sun is the greater among
the gods. And they said that the other planets are gods,
but that the sun and moon are the greatest of their gods.
You will find what they undoubtedly say, that the sun
governs the upper and lower world. All this you will find
in their books; and they speak of the condition of Abraham, and they declare further that Abraham was born and
educated in the land of fire worshippers. He there con-
tradicted their opinions, saying that there was another
operator besides the sun. And they offered their reasons
opposed to his, and among which they mentioned the
operations of the sun, which are manifest and which appear
to be seen throughout the universe.' But Abraham was cast
into chains because he refused to adore their sun, and after
that he was robbed of his goods, and by the king banished
into Canaan. They believed that the sun ruled the world,
that there was no god superior to him, and they adored
fire. Therefore, what else was fire than the sign or symbol
of the sun, and very consonant to his nature? And here,
I think, is seen the god of Nahor, son of Terah, referred
to in Genesis xxxi., 53 :—'The god of Abraham, the God

of Nahor, the god of their father, judge betwixt us.' Here, likewise, you have the foreign gods, which the ancients served in the time of Abraham, as the Sacred Scriptures testify, in Joshua XXIV., 2:—'And Joshua said unto all the people, Thus saith the Lord God of Israel, your fathers dwelt on the other side of the flood in the olden time, even Terah, the father of Abraham and the father of Nahor: and they served other gods.' Certainly before the Babylonian captivity also, and in the kingdom of Judea, those Pyratheia and the worship of fire existed, if Joseph Scaliger conjectures correctly in Catullus, when, in the sacred language, or that of the prophets, he says that the Pyratheia are called Chamanim.

"In II. Chronicles, XXXIV., 4, we find as follows in regard to Josiah, the king:—'And they broke down the altars of Baalim in his presence, and he broke into pieces the images that were sacred to him.' The images here in Hebrew are called Chamanim, and the Rabbins understand them to be effigies of the sun. For the sun and heat were called Chamha, thence Chamanim was used for the images, chapels, or Pyrathean consecrated to the sun. In Leviticus XXVI., 30, the words are as follows:—'I will destroy your high places, and cut down Chamanicem, that is, your images,' &c. The Hebrews understand that their idols were dedicated in honour of the sun. In that place in Leviticus and elsewhere Chamanim and other sacred rites borrowed from the Persians are reproved, and among these 'high places,' called Bamoth in Hebrew. It was a custom of the Persians to perform their sacred rites in the most high and elevated places, and in this way they offered sacrifice to heaven or Jove. Herodotus, in Clio, says 'it was their custom to ascend the most lofty summits of the mountains, and there immolate their victims to Jove, and calling by the name of Jove every circle of the heavens.' But it was a custom both of the Europeans and Asiatics to ascend the summits of mountains to worship Jove. Hence he was called Epakrios, or the Lofty.

"That Jupiter, with Herodotus, is Belus and Assyrius, for in that name he was called Jove in the most ancient theology of the Persians, as Berosus, Athenocles, and Simachus write. It is a question for the learned whether in the god Omanus, or Amanus, whom Strabo mentions, reference

may be had to Chamanim, or Hamanim. Scaliger thinks in
the affirmative, and he thence deduces Achæmenis and
Achæmeniss, who denote Persian extraction. Amanus was
indeed the sun, as Anaitis was the moon, and who were
called Diana and Venus. No one, however, is ignorant that
the Persians worshipped fire as a symbol of the sun, and
that is the reason why Datis, the captain of a ship under
Xerxes, left the island of Delos unharmed, inasmuch as it
was sacred to the sun, or Apollo. As to the other kind
of Chamanim, or effigy reduced to powder by King Josiah,
the following will be found in II. Kings, xxiii., 11, 'And
in process of time he removed the horses which the King
of Judah had given to the sun, in the entrance of the
temple of the Lord, near the tabernacle of Nathan-melech
the eunuch, who was a prince in the suburbs, and he burnt
the chariots of the sun in fire.' These also, perhaps, should
be called Chamanim, as Cimchi, Solomon Jarchi, and Levi
Ben Gershon explain that place concerning the horses and
chariot, that, while adoring the rising sun, they led them
in solemn pomp from the entrance of the temple to the
tabernacle of Nathan-melech. This more probably means the
molten images of the horses and chariots consecrated to the
sun, for, among the Persians, the horse was sacred to the
sun, and accustomed to be sacrificed to it. The same custom
was transplanted among the Grecians. In ancient times the
chariots were also dedicated to the same, as the swiftest of
swift gods. But their place was at the door of the True
God. The Jews worshipped the sun towards the east within
the vestibule of the door. Thus in Ezekiel viii., 14, 'And
behold, near the temple of the Lord, between the vestibule
and the altar, there were as if twenty-five men, whose backs
were towards the temple of the Lord, and their faces towards
the east, and they adored the sun in the east.' " *

From most of the classic authors, such as Homer,
Tibullus, Horace, Ovid, Euripides, Aristophanes, Virgil, &c.,
we gather that every Greek and Roman house had its altar
on which fire was ever burning. At night it was covered
up with ashes so as to reserve some of the wood for the
morrow and keep it gently and slowly smouldering. Day
by day, the first thing in the morning, the master of the

---

* Selden's Syrian Deities, Hausser's Translation.

house applied himself to the rousing up or rekindling of the fire, in order that it might be ready for the coming ceremonies and worship; in his absence from home this duty devolved upon his wife as his nearest relation. Writers tell us that the fire did not cease to burn until the family had altogether perished, and an extinguished hearth in early days meant the same thing as an extinguished family.

Nor was the keeping up of this fire a mere matter of unmeaning form, a simple custom to which no signification of any particular importance was attached; it was essentially connected with the people's most ancient and cherished religious beliefs. So serious a matter was it that even the particular kind of wood was specified. Virgil and Plutarch distinctly state that only certain trees ought to be used for such a purpose, and these were kept sacred and forbidden for other uses. The fire, according to Euripides and Ovid, must be kept pure—no polluted object might be cast into it, no offensive action might be performed in its presence.

As we remark in another place, there was one day in the year (March 1st in Rome) when all fires and lights were put out—but immediately renewed with the observation of many rites. The strictest rules had to be attended to on these occasions; it was forbidden to renew the fire from any remaining spark of the old—indeed it was essential to thoroughly extinguish every spark of the previous flame— neither might a spark be struck from flint and steel; only by the sun's rays or by rubbing two pieces of wood together might the new fire be started into being, for the fire was regarded as the representative of the sun—the greatest of lights and fires, and as such was adored. Well it was not unreasonable or to be wondered at, that men, for want of better knowledge, should render divine honours to that from which they received such benefits; they saw the light and heat of the sun pouring down upon the earth and in con- junction with the rain and dew, softening its crust, swelling and fructifying its seed and bringing forth from it food and nourishment for man and beast. And so they prayed as we read in the Orphic hymns: "Render us always flourishing, always happy, O fire: thou who art eternal, beautiful, ever young; thou who nourishest, thou who art rich, receive favourably these our offerings, and in return give us happiness and sweet health."

The fire seems to have been perpetually invoked; hardly a monument was made, hardly a household or business duty performed or engagement fulfilled, without a prayer to it; if a man left his home for a brief while, he worshipped the fire; when he returned, before he saluted his nearest relatives, the same duty was observed. Æschylus tells of Agamemnon returning from Troy, and instead of going to the temple and returning thanks to Jupiter, offering thanksgiving before the fire in his own house. Euripides, also, represents the dying Alcestis speaking to the fire: "Mistress, I go beneath the earth, and for the last time fall before thee, and address thee. Protect my infant children; give to my boy a tender wife, and to my daughter a noble husband. Let them not die, like their mother, before the time, but may they lead a long and happy life in their fatherland."

De Coulanges says "the sacred fire was a sort of providence in the family. Sacrifices were offered to it, and not merely was the flame supplied with wood, but upon the altar were poured wine, oil, incense and the fat of victims. The god graciously received these offerings and devoured them. Radiant with satisfaction, he rose above the altar, and lit up the worshipper with his brightness. Then was the moment for the suppliant humbly to invoke him and give heartfelt utterance to his prayer."

Corresponding with the "grace" of modern times, recited before and after meals, was the tribute of prayer and praise uttered by the ancient before his fire when he was about to partake of food and when he had satisfied his hunger. He went even further than the modern does, for before a particle of food was eaten a due proportion of meat and drink had to be poured out upon the altar and presented to the god. And when the flame rose up, they regarded it as the deity rearing himself in their midst and consuming what had been presented.

If we turn to the Sacred Books of the East we shall find how strong a hold this Fire Worship has upon the Hindoo mind, and the importance attached to a due observance of all points of ritual connected with it. In the "Laws of Manu" we find directions for his guidance extending to the most ordinary domestic necessities and some of which we cannot very well repeat in these pages. Some of his private necessities must not be satisfied in view of the fire but he must retire either into darkness or out of sight of it. "Let him not blow a fire with his mouth—Let him not throw any impure substance into the fire, let him not warm his feet at it—Let him not place fire under a bed or the like; nor step over it, nor place it when he sleeps at the footend of his bed—Let him keep his right arm uncovered in a place where a sacred fire is kept—A Brahmana who is impure most not touch with his hand a cow, a Brahmana, or fire; nor, being in good health, let him look at the luminaries in the sky while he is impure." Then again, "A Brahmana shall offer of the cooked food destined for the Vaisvadeva in the sacred domestic fire to the following deities: First to Agni, and next to Soma, then to both these gods conjointly, further to all the gods, and then to Dhanvautari, further to Kuhu (the goddess of the new moon day), to Anumati (the goddess of the full moon day), to Pragapati (the lord of creatures), to heaven and earth conjointly, and finally to Agni Svishtakrit (the fire which performs the sacrifice well)." And so on in many other places, in one of which the king is to behave like fire. "Let the king emulate the energetic action of Indra, of the sun, of the wind, of Yama, of Varuna, of the moon, of the fire, and of the earth. If he is ardent in wrath against criminals and endowed with brilliant energy, and destroys wicked vassals, then his character is said to resemble that of fire."

Turning to the Rig Veda we find "Hymns to Agni (the god of fire) and the Maruts (the storm gods)."

"1. Thou art called forth to this fair sacrifice for a draught of milk; with the Maruts come hither, O Agni!"

"2. No god, indeed, no mortal, is beyond the might of thee, the mighty one; with the Maruts come hither, O Agni?"

"3. Those who know of the great sky, the Visne Devas without guile; with those Maruts come hither, O Agni!"

"4. The wild ones who sing their song, unconquerable by force; with the Maruts come hither, O Agni!"

"5. Those who are brilliant, of awful shape, powerful, and devourers of foes; with the Maruts come hither, O Agni!"

"6. They who in heaven are enthroned as gods, in the light of the firmament; with the Maruts come hither, O Agni!"

"7. They who shoot with their darts across the sea with might; with the Maruts come hither, O Agni!"

"9. I pour out to thee for the early draught the sweet juice of Soma; with the Maruts come hither, O Agni!"

Another one says:—"O Agni, thou art the life, thou art the patron of man. In return for our prayers, bestow glory and riches on the father of a family who now addresses thee. Agni, thou art a wise protector and a father; to thee we owe life, we are of thy household."

De Coulanges says:—"So the hearth-god was, as in Greece, a tutelary deity. Men asked of him abundance, and that the earth might be productive. He was prayed to for health, and that a man might long enjoy the light and arrive at old age like the sun at his setting. Even wisdom is demanded, and pardon for sin. For as in Greece the fire-god was essentially pure, so not only was the Brahmin forbidden to throw anything filthy into his fire, but he might not even warm his feet at it. The guilty man, also, as in Greece, might not approach his own hearth before he was purified from the stain he had contracted.

Assuredly the Greeks did not borrow this religion from the Hindoos, nor the Hindoos from the Greeks; but Greeks, Italians, and Hindoos, belonged to one and the same race, and their ancestors at a very early period had lived together in Central Asia. There they had learnt this creed, and established their rites. When the tribes gradually moved further away from one another, they transported this religion with them, the one to the banks of the Ganges, and the others to the Mediterranean. Afterwards, some learnt to worship Brahma, others Zeus, and others again Janus; but all had preserved as a legacy the earlier religion which they had practised at the common cradle of the race.

It is remarkable that in all sacrifices, even in those offered to Zeus or to Athene, it was always to the fire that the first invocation was made. At Olympia assembled Greece offered her first sacrifice to the hearth-fire, and the second to Zeus. Similarly at Rome, the first to be adored was always Vesta, who was nothing else but the fire. And so we read in the hymns of the Veda: "Before all gods, Agni must be invoked. We will pronounce thy holy name before that of all the other immortals. O Agni, whatever be the god we honour by our sacrifice, to thee is the holocaust offered."

It was not that Jupiter and Brahma had not acquired a much greater importance in the minds of men, but it was remembered that the fire was much older than the gods. When the populations of Greece and Italy had learnt to represent their Gods as persons, and had given each a proper name and a human shape, the old worship of the fire was similarly modified. The sacred fire was called Vesta. The common noun was made a proper name, and a legend by degrees attached to it. They even went so far as to represent the fire in statues under the features of a woman, the gender of the noun having determined the sex of the deity.

Vesta, in mythology, was one of the principal deities of the Pagans. Those who have diligently investigated the religion of the Pythagorean philosophers pretend that by Vesta they meant the universe, to which they ascribed a soul, and which they worshipped as the sole divinity sometime under the name of το παν, the whole, and sometimes under the appellation of μονος, unity. However, fabulous history records two goddesses under the name of Vesta; one the mother of Saturn, and wife of Cœlum, and the other the daughter of Saturn, by his wife Rhea. The first was Terra, or the Earth, called also Cybele, and derived her name Vesta, according to some, from clothing, because the earth is clothed, *vestitur*, with plants and fruits, or, according to Ovid, from the stability of the earth because *stat vi terra sua*, or it supports itself. Hence the first oblations in all sacrifices were offered to her, because whatsoever is sacrificed springs from the earth; and the Greeks both began and concluded their sacrifices with Vesta, because they esteemed her the mother of all gods.

The second was Fire, and Vesta whose power was exercised about altars and houses, derives her name, according to Cicero, from fire or hearth. Accordingly the poets frequently use Vesta for fire or flame; as they do Jupiter for air, Ceres for corn, &c. An image of Vesta, to which they sacrificed every day, was placed before the doors of the houses at Rome; and the places where these statues were erected were called *vestibula*, from Vesta. This goddess was a virgin, and so great an admirer of virginity, that when Jupiter her brother gave her leave to ask what she would, she besought that she might always be a virgin, and have the first oblations in all sacrifices.

This goddess is called by Horace *æterna Vesta*, and it was in honour of her that Numa erected a temple at Rome, and dedicated virgins to keep a perpetual fire upon her altars. One way of representing this goddess, it is said, was in the habit of a matron, holding in her right hand a flambeau or lamp, and sometimes a Palladium or small Victory.

The worship of Vesta and of fire was brought from Phrygia into Italy by Æneas and the other Trojans who resorted thither. To this purpose Virgil observes that Æneas, before he left the palace of his father, had taken away the fire from the sacred hearth. The name Vesta was synonymous with the Chaldean and Persian Avesta and hence Zoroaster gave to his book on the worship of fire, the name of Avesta or Abesta, *i.e.*, the custody of fire.

The Vestals were the virgins in Ancient Rome, consecrated to the service of the goddess Vesta, whose worship, we have said, was brought into Italy by Æneas, and one of their special duties was the watching of the sacred fire, the going out of which was visited upon them with such severe whipping. This fire, which they had to watch so jealously and carefully, was neither on an altar nor on a hearth, but in little earthen vessels with two handles, called *capeduncula*. It was held a pledge of the empire of the world. If it went out, it was judged a very unlucky prognostic, and was to be expiated with infinite ceremonies. Among the Romans, Festus tells us, it was only to be rekindled by rubbing a kind of wood proper for the purpose. But among the Greeks, Plutarch, in his life of Numa, observes, it was to be rekindled by exposing some inflammable matter in the centre of a concave vessel held to the sun. It is to be noted, the Romans were not the only people who kept the perpetual fire of Vesta, in imitation of the celestial fires; but the Greeks were possessed with the same superstition; particularly the Delphians, Athenians, Tenedians, Argives, Rhodians, Cyzicenians, Milesians, Ephesians, &c.

Magi, or Magians, was the title which the ancient Persians gave to their wise men and philosophers. Whatever may be the origin of the word, and upon this great diversity of opinion seems to have prevailed, it corresponds with the σοφοι among the Greeks; sapientes among the Latins; Druids among the Gauls; Gynosophists among the Indians; and prophets, priests among the Egyptians.

Plato, Apuleius, Laertius, and others agree that the philosophy of the Magi related principally to the worship of the gods; they were the persons who were to offer prayers, supplications and sacrifices, as if the gods would be heard by them alone.

They teach their doctrine concerning the nature and origin of the gods, says Laertius, whom they think to be fire, earth, and water; they reject the use of pictures and images, and reprobate the opinion that the gods are male and female; they discourse to the people concerning justice; they think it impious to consume dead bodies with fire; they all practise divination and prophecy, pretending that the gods appear to them; they forbid the use of ornaments in dress; they clothe themselves in a white robe; they make use of the ground as their bed, of herbs, cheese and bread for food, and of a reed for their staff. Strabo also relates, that there were in Cappadocia a great number of Magi, who were called "Pyrethi," or worshippers of fire, and many temples of the Persian gods, in the midst of which were altars attended by priests, who daily renewed the sacred fire, accompanying the ceremony with music.

The chief doctrine of the Magi was, that there were two principles, one of which was the cause of all good, and the other the cause of all evil. The former was represented by light, and the latter by darkness, as their truest symbols; and of the composition of these two they supposed that all things in the world were made. The good god they always worshipped before fire, as being the cause of light, and especially before the sun, as being in their opinion the most perfect fire, and causing the most perfect light; and for this reason they had in all their temples fire constantly burning on altars erected in them for that purpose. Before these sacred fires, they performed all their public acts of devotion, as they likewise practised their private devotions before their private fires in their own houses. Such were the tenets of this sect when Smerdis, who was the principal leader of it, having usurped the crown after the death of Cambyses, was slain by seven princes of Persia; and many of the Magians, who adhered to him, shared likewise the same fate. In consequence of this event, those who adopted the sentiments of this sect were called, by way of derision, Magians, from *mige-gush*, which signified, in the language of

the country then in use, one that had his ears cropped.
The whole sect of the Magians would soon have sunk into
utter extinction if it had not, in a few years after this
period, been revived and reformed by Zoroaster. This celebrated philosopher, called by the Persians Zerdusht or
Zaratusht, began about the thirty-sixth year of the reign of
Darius to restore and reform the Magian system of religion.
He was not only excellently skilled in all the learning of
the East that prevailed in his time, but likewise thoroughly
versed in the Jewish religion, and in all the sacred writings
of the Old Testament that were then extant, whence some
have inferred that he was a native Jew both by birth and
profession; and that he had been servant to one of the
prophets, probably Ezekiel or Daniel. He made his first
appearance in Media, in the city of Xiz, afterwards called
Aderbijan, as some say; or according to others, in Ecbatana,
afterwards Tauris. Instead of admitting the existence of two
first causes with the Magians, he introduced a principle
superior to them both—one supreme God, who created both
these, and out of these two produced, according to his
sovereign pleasure, everything else.

Zoroaster caused fire temples to be erected wherever he
came: for having feigned that he was taken up into heaven,
and there instructed in the doctrines he taught by God
himself, out of the midst of a great and most bright flame
of fire, he taught his followers that fire was the truest
shekinah of the divine presence; that the sun being the
most perfect fire, God had there the throne of his glory,
and the residence of his divine presence in a peculiar manner; and next to this in our elementary fire; and, therefore,
he ordered them to direct all their worship to God, first
towards the sun, which they called Mithra, and next towards
their sacred fires; and when they came before these fires
to worship, they always approached them on the west side,
that having their faces towards them, and also towards the
rising sun at the same time, they might direct their worship
towards both. And in this posture they always performed
every act of their worship. Zoroaster also pretended that he
brought some of the heavenly fire with him on his return
and placed it on the altar of the first fire temple, which
he erected at Xiz, in Media, whence it was propagated to
all the rest; and on this account their priests carefully
watched it and never suffered it to be extinguished.

Zoroaster, having assumed the character of a divine prophet and reformer of religion, retired into a cave, devoting himself to prayer and meditation, where he composed the book called the Zend, in which his pretended revelations were contained. From Media he removed into Bactria; and he went also into India among the Brachmans, and having acquired all their knowledge in mathematics, philosophy and astronomy, returned and communicated the knowledge to his Magians; and thus they became famous for their skill in these sciences; so that a learned man and a Magian were equivalent terms. The vulgar conceived of them as persons actuated and inspired by supernatural powers; and hence those who pretended to wicked and diabolical acts, assumed the name of Magians; and the term Magician acquired its evil meaning. However, this distinguished knowledge was confined to those who were by way of eminence, the Magi, or the priests; who, like those of the Jews, being of the same tribe, appropriated their learning to their own families. These priests were distributed into three orders, viz.: the inferior priests, who conducted the ordinary ceremonies of religion; the superintendents who governed them and presided over the sacred fire; and the archimagus, or high-priest, who possessed supreme authority over the whole order; and their churches or temples were also of three sorts, parochial or oratories, in which the people performed their devotions, and where the sacred fire was kept only in lamps; fire-temples, in which fire was kept continually burning on a sacred altar, where the higher order of the Magi directed the public devotions, and the people assembled to perform magical incantations, hear interpretations of dreams, and practise other superstitions; and lastly, the fire-temple in which the archimagus resided, which was visited by the people at certain seasons with peculiar solemnity, and to which it was deemed an indispensable duty for every one to repair at least once in his life. Zoroaster at length carried his religious system to the royal court at Susa, and made Darius a proselyte, together with most of the great men of the kingdom.

THE END.

H

PHALLIC SERIES

CR. 8VO, VELLUM, 7/6 EACH.

Only a *very limited number*, privately printed.

PHALLICISM.—A Description of the Worship of **Lingam-Yoni** in various parts of the World, and in different Ages, with an Account of Ancient and Modern Crosses, particularly of the **Crux Ansata** (or Handled Cross) and other Symbols connected with the Mysteries of **Sex Worship.**

Only a few copies to be sold with sets at 7/6, or separately, 10/6.

OPHIOLATREIA.—An Account of the Rites and Mysteries connected with the Origin, Rise, and Development of **Serpent Worship** in various parts of the World, enriched with Interesting Traditions, and a full description of the celebrated Serpent Mounds and Temples, the whole forming an exposition of one of the phases of **Phallic, or Sex Worship.**

PHALLIC OBJECTS, MONUMENTS AND REMAINS; Illustrations of the Rise and Development of the **Phallic Idea** (Sex Worship), and its embodiment in Works of Nature and Art. *Etched Frontispiece.*

CULTUS ARBORUM.—A Descriptive Account of **Phallic Tree Worship,** with illustrative Legends, Superstitious Usages, &c.; exhibiting its Origin and Development amongst the Eastern and Western Nations of the World, from the earliest to modern times.

www.ingramcontent.com/pod-product-compliance
Lightning Source LLC
Chambersburg PA
CBHW030545270326
41927CB00008B/1527